Acclaim for KATE BORNSTEIN'S

GENDER OUTLAW

"While Bornstein covers an incredible range—from the 'nuts and bolts' of her surgery to more abstract musings on a brave new gender-free world—the book never stops fascinating. [She offers us] an abundance of questions—thoughtful, disarming, revelatory questions. *Gender Outlaw* is an invitation to a dialogue, and it's a conversation well worth having." —*Ms.*

"Kate Bornstein argues eloquently and passionately for scrapping the categories of women and men. Agree. Disagree. Read it!"
—Leslie Feinberg, author of *Stone Butch Blues*

"The first book of gender theory written by a transgendered person . . . includes countless insights, trenchant cultural analysis, and generous wit. . . . [It] will surely become a classic." —*Washington Blade*

"[Bornstein is on the] leading edge of contemporary debate about sexual identity and gender. [She] asks fundamental and challenging questions about what it means to be a man or woman in our society."
—*San Francisco Chronicle*

"*Gender Outlaw* is an eye-opening book, combining the emotional force of a coming-of-age story with a savvy cultural critique." —*Out*

"A radical document." —*The Nation*

"Kate is an orgasm on two legs. Reading this book gives me a heart orgasm, and it could give you one too! *Gender Outlaw* is a great work of love." —Annie Sprinkle, performance artist

"Kate Bornstein is a fierce and funny voice on the front lines of gender and sexual identity. Her wise heart and wild imagination challenge us to really own our bodies, our desires, our dreams."
—Tim Miller, performance artist

KATE BORNSTEIN

GENDER OUTLAW

Kate Bornstein divides her time between the San Francisco Bay Area and Seattle. Her stage work includes her solo performance pieces *The Opposite Sex Is Neither* and *Virtually Yours*. When not writing or performing, Kate can be found cuddling with Gwydyn, following the adventures of Hothead Paisan, or prowling the Net, playing vampire role-playing games and *Star Trek*.

KATE BORNSTEIN

GENDER
OUTLAW

On Men,
Women,
and the Rest of Us

VINTAGE BOOKS

A Division of Random House, Inc.   New York

FIRST VINTAGE BOOKS EDITION, MAY 1995

Copyright © 1994 by Routledge
Afterword copyright © 1995 by Kate Bornstein

The author gratefully acknowledges the permission
of *Issues Monthly* (February 1991) to reprint "Nuts and Bolts"
and the "Lesbian Thing" in this volume.

Photo credits: pp. ii, 226: Dona Ann McAdams;
p. 112: Glenn Tonneson; p. 142: Ingrid White; pp. 146, 168: Jill Posener;
p. 166: David Harrison; p. 224: Janet Van Ham.

Library of Congress Cataloging-in-Publication Data
Bornstein, Kate, 1948–
Gender outlaw: on men, women, and the rest of us /
Kate Bornstein — 1st Vintage Books ed.
p. cm.
Originally published : New York : Routledge, 1994.
Includes the text of the play, Hidden: a gender.
Includes bibliographical references.
ISBN 0-679-75701-5
1. Bornstein, Kate, 1948– —Psychology. 2. Transsexuals.
3. Gender identity. 4. Sex change. 5. Sex (Psychology)
6. Lesbians. I. Bornstein, Kate, 1948–
Hidden, a gender. II. Title.
HQ77.9.B67 1995
305.3—dc20
94-23477
CIP

Manufactured in the United States of America
10 9 8

This book is dedicated to my friend and teacher, John Emigh, who taught me about laughter and acting, who showed me it was OK to break some rules and to follow some others, who responded to my gender change with both respect and a good sense of humor, and who encouraged me to continue working in theater when I was sure I'd have to give it up. Bless you and thank you, John—you've always asked me challenging questions.

In Loving Memory of:

Doris Fish

"Tippi"

Lou Sullivan

Tedde Matthews

John Payne

Leland Moss

Ethyl Eichelberger

Charles Ludlam

Kelly

Christine Jorgensen

and

Billy Tipton

come see what's on the inside!

GENDER OUTLAW

LIFE WITH FATHER
AND MOTHER
BEGAN FOR

ALBERT
HERMAN

MARCH
15"

first things first

I keep trying to integrate my life. I keep trying to make all the pieces into one piece. As a result, my identity becomes my body which becomes my fashion which becomes my writing style. Then I perform what I've written in an effort to integrate my life, and that becomes my identity, after a fashion.

My mother was so proud to have given birth to a son. Today, our friendship is more than either mother-son or mother-daughter.

<< 1 >>

TRANSGENDER STYLE
Some Fashion Tips

People are starting to ask me about fashion. I love that! Maybe they think the doctor
sewed in some fashion sense during my genital conversion surgery.

I see fashion as a proclamation or manifestation of identity, so, as long as
identities are important, fashion will continue to be important. The link
between fashion and identity begins to get real interesting, however, in
the case of people who don't fall clearly into a culturally-recognized
identity—people like me. My identity as a transsexual lesbian whose
female lover is becoming a man is manifest in my fashion statement; both
my identity and fashion are based on collage. You know—a little bit from
here, a little bit from there? Sort of a cut-and-paste thing.

And that's the style of this book. It's a
transgendered style, I suppose. I can see it
in the work of Susan Stryker, Sandy Stone,
David Harrison...the list goes on and on.

But the need for a recognizable identity, and the need to belong to a
group of people with a similar identity—these are driving forces in our
culture, and nowhere is this more evident than in the areas of gender

and sexuality. Hence the clear division between fashion statements of male and female, between the fashions of queer and straight.

In my case, however, it's not so clear. I identify as neither male nor female, and now that my lover is going through his gender change, it turns out I'm neither straight nor gay. What I've found as a result of this borderline life is that the more fluid my identity has become, and the less demanding my own need to belong to the camps of male, female, gay or straight, the more playful and less dictatorial my fashion has become—as well as my style of self-expression.

> Will the identification with a transgendered writing style produce an identification with a transgendered experience?

Anyone who knows fashion will tell you that the operative word is *accessorize!* That's how I dress in the morning. That's how I shift from one phase of my life to the next—first I try on the accessories. And that's also part of the style of this book: I've added some accessories here and there to spice it up a bit.

Welcome to my runway!

sorting seeds

The very first task that Psyche had to accomplish in her search to be reunited with her lover, Eros, was to sort, by type, a roomful of seeds. According to the myth, these seeds covered the floor, and rose to nearly the height of the ceiling. I spent the first thirty years of my life sorting out the cultural seeds of gender and sexuality.

In the backyard of our house on the Jersey Shore.
I'm about four years old.

« 2 »

THE HARD PART

*The novel being dead, there is no point to
writing made up stories. Look at the French
who will not and the Americans who cannot.
Look at me who ought not, if only because I
exist entirely outside the usual human experience...outside and yet wholly relevant for I
am the New Woman whose astonishing history is a poignant amalgam of vulgar dreams
and knife-sharp realities (shall I ever be free
of the dull lingering pain that is my peculiar
glory, the price so joyously paid for being
Myra Breckinridge, whom no man may possess except on her...my terms!).*
  —Gore Vidal, *Myra Breckinridge*, 1974

The hard part was sorting it all out. The hard part was taking a good
look at everyone else and the way they looked at the world, which was a
lot different from the way *I* was looking at the world!

There are some transsexuals who agree with
the way I look at the world, and quite a few
who are really angry with me for writing
this stuff. Every transsexual I know went

through a gender transformation for different reasons, and there are as many truthful experiences of gender as there are people who think they have a gender.

I know I'm not a man—about that much I'm very clear, and I've come to the conclusion that I'm probably not a woman either, at least not according to a lot of people's rules on this sort of thing. The trouble is, we're living in a world that insists we be one or the other—a world that doesn't bother to tell us exactly what one or the other *is*.

When I was a kid, everyone else seemed to know they were boys or girls or men or women. That's something I've never known; not then, not today. I never got to say to the grownups, "Hold on there—just what is it about me that makes you think I'm a little boy?" As a kid, I just figured I was the crazy one; I was the one who really had some serious defect.

All my life, my non-traditional gender identity had been my biggest secret, my deepest shame. It's not that I didn't want to talk about this with someone; it's just that I never saw anything in the culture that encouraged me to talk about my feeling that I was the wrong gender. When I was growing up, people who lived cross-gendered lives were pressured into hiding deep within the darkest closets they could find. Those who came out of their closets were either studied under a microscope, ridiculed in the tabloids, or made exotic in the porn books, so it paid to hide. It paid to lie. That was probably the most painful part of it: the lying to friends and family and lovers, the pretending to be someone I wasn't. Going through a gender change is not the easiest thing in the world to do, but I went through it because I was so tired of all the lies and secrets.

It was a strange kind of lie. It was a lie by action—I was always acting out something that everyone assumed I was. I wonder what it would have been like if someone had come along and in a quite friendly manner had asked, "Well, young one, what do you think you are: a boy or a girl?" What would it have been like not to have been afraid of getting hit because of some wrong answer? See, "sex changes" never were an appropriate topic of conversation—not at the dining table, not in the locker room, not over a casual lunch in a crowded restaurant.

Nowadays, I try to make it easier for people to ask questions. I tell people that I've never been hurt by an honest question, and that's true: it's a cruel opinion that hurts, not a question. But people still don't ask questions easily; maybe that has something to do with manners or etiquette. Folks seem to naturally back off from inquiring as to the nature of someone's—my—gender. It seems to need some special setting. Like in my living room, or on television, or from behind a podium at some university. It's "good manners" to say and ask nothing, and that's sad. But the children still ask.

Two days after my lover and I appeared on The Donahue Show, the five-year-old child of our next door neighbor came up to me and asked me, "So, are you a boy or a girl?" We'd been living next door to these folks for over two years.

"I'm a girl who used to be a boy," I replied. She was delighted with that answer and told me I'd looked very pretty on television. I thanked her and we smiled at each other and went about our days. I love it that kids will just ask.

Adults don't ask. Adults are afraid to ask, "What *are* you?" so we ask "What do you *do*?"...in hopes of getting a clue to someone's identity—gender identity seems to be an unspeakable thing in our culture, just as names are considered unspeakable in some other cultures. By the same token, we hardly ever ask outright "What kind of sex do you like?" When it comes to work, we can ask. When it comes to sex and gender, we're supposed to observe discreetly and draw our own conclusions.

Instead of asking directly, adults look in roundabout ways for answers to their questions about me and my people. Like reading transsexual and transvestite pornography which, judging by much of its content, must be written by people who have never met one of us, but who have certainly fantasized about us.

> There's this entire wonderful underground genre of erotica. You may have seen some of the titles, they're terrific, like **He's Her Sister!** (Get it?) Or **Transvestite Marriage** or **Transvestite Trap**. My personal favorites were **Captive In Lace**, and **They Made Him Love It!**

Reading those stories came in handy when I was doing phone sex for a living, because a lot of the men calling in wanted to be cross-dressed as women, or they wanted to know what it would be like to be a woman and have sex with another woman—guys want to know that sort of thing. They want to know, "what do lesbians *do* with one another." It's a sad question really: it shows how little thought they give to exactly what pleases a woman.

> There's another whole group of people who really **like** gender ambiguity, it turns them on. I remember a group of sailors in the audience on **The Geraldo Show**. After it was announced who and what I was, they kept on looking at me, they kept on wanting something. I could feel

> their eyes traveling up and down my sur-
> gically-constructed, hormonally-enhanced
> woman's body. What's the pull? What is it
> about a sexually-blended, gender-bended
> body that lights those flames? I know it
> gets me going!

For the most part, people cautiously observe and don't ask questions, and there are plenty of opportunities in today's world to look at people like me. The talk show ratings go way up during sweeps month when they trot out the transsexuals and the cross-dressers. Then there are the drag shows and the female impersonator spectacles—even though we began them for our own entertainment and enjoyment, their wide-spread popularity seems to grow and grow; you've probably got one of those shows in your city, or in a nearby town. Comedy skits, like "It's Pat" (a skit based on a person whose gender is not clear) on *Saturday Night Live* are real popular. I'll have more to say about that later.

If I look past the ghettos of the drag bars and standup joints, both popular music and cinema reflect my transsexual face back to me. Glance discreetly, if you will, at some of the brightest deities in our cultural heavens. At this writing, some friends of mine are truly interested in seeing if Michael Jackson (all his other issues aside) will actually become Diana Ross. I've heard bets being placed on the gender of some of Madonna's lovers in some of her videos. And what really made *The Crying Game* the smash hit that it was? It's interesting that we can ask questions about transgender issues when there's some distance between us and the person we're asking about—we just don't ask directly.

There's a lot of writing about gender now. I keep reading the magazine articles, the newspaper columns, and the text books, pre- and post-modern. I read, watch, and listen to all the ads and commercials. You can learn a lot about gender from those commercials. I've also been watching the talk shows, listening to the call-in programs, and browsing the electronic bulletin boards. When I was very young, growing up in the 50s, I read the medical texts, devoured the tabloids, and hoarded the pornography—because I was intensely interested in me and my people. I was scared, though, shaking scared, to see what I might actually find out. But I couldn't stop reading.

> See, I was a lonely, frightened little fat kid who felt there was something deeply wrong with me because I didn't feel like I was the gender I'd been assigned. I felt there was something wrong with me, something sick and twisted inside me, something very very bad about me. And everything I read backed that up.

The possibility missed by most of the texts prior to the last few years, and by virtually all the various popular media, is this: the culture may not simply be creating roles for naturally-gendered people, the culture may in fact be *creating* the gendered people. In other words, the culture may be creating gender. No one had ever hinted at that, and so, standing outside a "natural" gender, I thought I was some monster, and that it was all my fault.

In living along the borders of the gender frontier, I've come to see the gender system created by this culture as a particularly malevolent and divisive construct, made all the more dangerous by the seeming inability of the culture to *question* gender, its own creation. The studies conducted by the duly-appointed representatives of the culture were still done on the basis of observation, not conversation. I want this book to begin to reverse that trend. I want this book to be the conversation I always wanted as I was growing up, and never had the chance to have.

The time for discreet and distant observation of transgendered lives seems to be coming to an end. There's more and more evidence that transgendered folks are making a place for themselves in the culture. I'm writing this book, for example, and it's getting published because there's been a shift. Up until the last few years, all we'd be able to write *and get published* were our autobiographies, tales of women trapped in the bodies of men or men pining away in the bodies of women. Stories by and about brave people who'd lived their lives hiding deep within a false gender—and who, after much soul-searching, decided to change their gender, and spent the rest of their days hiding deep within *another* false gender. That's what we could get published about ourselves—the romantic stuff which set in stone our image as long-suffering, not the challenging stuff. And it always seemed that the people who would write *about* us either had some ax to grind or point to prove, or they'd been hurt and needed someone to blame it on. People like Janice Raymond, Catherine Millot, and Robert Stoller have ultimately perpetuated the myth that transgendered people are malevolent, mentally ill, or monsters. We got left holding the cultural bag. We ended up wearing the cultural hand-me-downs.

But there's another kind of trans(gressive)gender experience going on in this culture, and nowadays we're writing our own chronicles of these times. Our stories all tie together, our stories overlap; and you can hear lots about me in the stories of other transgendered people. My story weaves through Caroline Cossey's story. My story lies within the story of late historian Louis Sullivan. Christine Jorgensen and Renee Richards wrote chapters of my story in their autobiographies. Sandy Stone teaches her story, my story, our story in any number of her classes. Rachel Pollack paints it into her tarot cards. Christine Beatty belts it out in heavy metal and whispers it in her poetry. Melanie Phillips makes it available in on-line cyberspace. Leslie Feinberg travels back and forth across the country to make our story heard in the political arena. Loren Cameron captures it in his black-and-white stills. Kristienne Clarke brings us into her made-for-television films. David Harrison performs our story live on stage, Wednesdays through Sundays. We're all of us speaking in our own transgendered voice these days: editor and publisher JoAnn Roberts, essayist and fiction writer James Green, activist and writer Susan Stryker, publishers Dallas Denny and Davina Anne Gabriel, poet Rikki Ann Wilchins, poet and essayist Max Valerio, publisher Marissa Sheryl Lynn, playwright and composer Omewenne Grimstone, performance artist Celie Edwards—the list keeps growing. We're talking to each other in meeting rooms, through newsletters and journals, and on electronic bulletin boards. It's an exciting time, here at the beginning of a movement. It's a time when we've begun to put down the cultural baggage. We've begun sewing sequins onto our cultural hand-me-downs.

My voice on this subject is not representative of all transgendered people. But when a minority group has been silent for as long as we have, as disjointed as we have been, the tendency is for those in the majority to listen to the loud ones when they first speak up; and to believe that we speak for the entire group. More important than my point of view, than any single point of view however, is that people begin to question gender.

The voices of transgendered people are now being raised in concert with the voices of more and more people who are writing their work based on what we have to say. Suzanne Kessler, Wendy McKenna, Marjorie Garber, Jennie Livingston, Judith Butler, Wendy Chapkis, Anne Bolin, Walter Williams, Holly Devor, Pat Califia, and Shannon Bell are all asking great questions and making room for us to respond.

I've taken as much care as I could to encourage questions in this book, especially questions about my conclusions. I hope that soon after this book is published I'll have some more questions. Questions are the hard part.

INTERLUDE

Nuts and Bolts

On the Surgical Process

Issues: *All right. We'd like to start with the biological/technical questions, the "nuts and bolts," as it were...*

Kate: [laughing]...I bolted from mine, that's for sure...

Issues: *...could you talk a little bit about the entire process of the surgery, and how it's done?*

Kate: It's a long process. It requires a year to two years of therapy, and then another therapist has to validate your therapist's opinion, for you to be qualified to go to a surgeon and say, "See, they think I'm a girl." During that time you can start hormones.

Before surgery you need to do what's called a "Life Test," which is living as another gender for at least a year, sometimes two years.

Issues: *What does that mean?*

Kate: Day and night. Before any kind of genital reassignment surgery. In other words, if *you* were going to do this, you'd have to live as a man for a year to two years to see if you could function socially, if you could make a living. For example, in *Hidden: A Gender*, the character Justin Bond plays [Herculine Barbin] couldn't function socially or economically as a man.

And so that would have been discovered and they would have said, "Hey, look. Give it up. Go back." And some people cannot get it together to function one way or the other. So you live that test, and then you go through with genital surgery. I know mostly about male-to-female surgery. There are two female-to-male techniques. Both are fine, except that sometimes they're not cosmetically up to snuff, so to speak.

Issues: *I was going to ask whether women can become men, because a lot more of the sex changes you hear about are men becoming women.*

Kate: Ah, the qualifier is that you *hear* about it; it's about 50-50.

Issues: *Where does the penis come from?*

Kate: Well, in one technique they take a skin graft, either from the inner thigh or the belly, literally roll it up, and attach it at the top of the thigh and the bottom of the belly. Then the patient has to lie in bed for four weeks or so while this heals up, to make sure the blood is going fine. So you've basically got what looks like a suitcase handle. They then remove one end from the thigh, so the suitcase handle is hanging down from the bottom of the belly. They don't have a way to extend the urethra through this penis, so the man must pee through the same urethral opening he had when he was a woman. Some men keep their vaginas, some have their vaginas partially sewn up.

Issues: *Okay. So what about men to women?*

Kate: The most common technique is the one I had: it's called "penile inversion." They lay the penis out, and make an incision down the length of it, pull the skin open, scrape out the spongy stuff, being very careful not to disturb the blood vessels and nerves. The scrotal sac is laid open, the testicles are removed and become compost, I guess [general laughter]. So then they take the tip of the penis and start pushing it in. Kind of like turning a sock inside-out. Everyone has this natural cavity, right, so they just push it in...

Issues: *They invert it.*

Kate: Yah, exactly. So that the outside of the penis becomes the walls of the new vagina. The tip of the penis functions in the position of a cervix. They create a kind of clitoris, using the spongy material from the perineum. And then they hope for the best. The real tricky part of the surgery is the urethra. You're catheterized, because if you can't pee, you die. So that's real important. And they place this big pack in there while everything heals for about five days, and then they remove the pack and you have to keep dilating your new vagina by putting this little balloon thing in, and pumping it up, and letting it dilate for about twenty minutes, five or six times a day.

One of the comic things which you're told about before surgery, which is so frightening, but funny in retrospect, is that when the pack has been in there, it's pushed up against this new urethral opening, and the catheter's been pushing it, so the urethral opening is pushed over to the side, so you don't know in which direction you're going to pee when you finally pee. So when I sat down to pee, it shot straight up in the air, and I was like, "Oh noooooooo!" But eventually it gets itself into the right position and you pee in the right direction.

There's a doctor at Stanford who performs this penile inversion technique who takes a section, about half an inch, of intestine, which is a mucus membrane, and also grafts that in there, so that it will lubricate, because it is, in fact, membranous tissue. I don't lubricate, so if I'm going to have any kind of penetration I need lubrication. The disadvantage to that technique is that it never stops lubricating, so you're kind of always wet and sloppy [smiles]. Which doesn't *have* to be a disadvantage.

Issues: *How much did all this cost?*

Kate: Remember, this was 1985-86: it was four thousand dollars for the nine days in the hospital, and four thousand dollars to the doctor. Then there was the round trip air fare, it was in Colorado…there's lots of fees involved in this. Blue Cross ended up paying for it. It took a while to process because of a computer fuck-up. They had put in "genital surgery" as a category, and they had my gender listed as female. Well, the only category that the computer could find vaguely near genital surgery was circumcision, and when it saw *circumcision* and *female*, it created a loop that it couldn't get out of. So it just spun around in the computer for a while.

On Hormones

Issues: *So this actual surgery happens after taking the hormones for a while? It's the last step?*

Kate: It's what they consider the final step, yah. And what happened with me was I got my surgery about seven months after I'd started taking hormones, because the hormones have different effects on people. Yes, they can cause breast growth, but this [referring to her chest] mostly grew after surgery. What happened with me is that my penis started shrinking incredibly while I was taking hormones. And the doctor said, "If I don't do the surgery now, we're going to have to add a skin graft from your butt or your thigh, so that you can have some kind of depth." I'd already told him that I didn't need much depth; [smiles] that wasn't what I was concerned with.

Issues: *What other effects did the hormones have?*

Kate: They changed the texture of my skin—my skin's a lot softer. They caused breast growth. I'm on a hormonal regimen now of what they would give most women after a hysterectomy, who still have a uterus. I take Premarin every day, which is estrogen, and then seven days a month I take progesterone.

Issues: *You're going to be taking that forever?*

Kate: Forever. Unless I want to go through menopause again....I went through all the "classic symptoms" of menopause when I was getting onto hormones initially. While I was still producing my own testosterone, I had to take these massive doses of estrogen to overcome that. I'd sit at my desk at work and cry a lot. And now, I've got seven days a month of raging PMS. The only thing I don't ever do is have cramps or bleed. But I get the water retention, the mood swings, and all that.

On Orgasms

Issues: *What is actually stimulated during orgasm? And where is it?*

Kate: There are different kinds of orgasm. My vaginal walls are more sensitive than your vaginal walls, your clitoris is more sensitive than my clitoris. I can be stimulated to clitoral orgasm. That's a lot of fun. Actually much more so than with a vaginal orgasm. It's been changing. But I can have a vaginal orgasm just by the stimulation of the vaginal walls. That's kind of nifty, too. I do have a lack of sensation in my labia. I can feel pressure, but the surface of the skin does not have any sensation. So there was a certain amount of nerve damage there.

My Bar Mitzvah: March 4, 1961, "Today I am a man."

NAMING ALL THE PARTS

For the first thirty-or-so years of my life, I didn't listen, I didn't ask questions, I didn't talk, I didn't deal with gender—I avoided the dilemma as best I could. I lived frantically on the edge of my white male privilege, and it wasn't 'til I got into therapy around the issue of my transsexualism that I began to take apart gender and really examine it from several sides. As I looked at each facet of gender, I needed to fix it with a definition, just long enough for me to realize that each definition I came up with was entirely inadequate and needed to be abandoned in search of deeper meaning.

> Definitions have their uses in much the same way that road signs make it easy to travel: they point out the directions. But you don't get where you're going when you just stand underneath some sign, waiting for it to tell you what to do.

I took the first steps of my journey by trying to define the phenomenon I was daily becoming.

> There's a real simple way to look at gender: Once upon a time, someone drew a line in the sands of a culture and proclaimed with great self-importance, "On this side, you are a man; on the other side, you are a woman." It's time for the winds of change to blow that line away. Simple.

Gender means *class*. By calling gender a system of classification, we can dismantle the system and examine its components. Suzanne Kessler and Wendy McKenna in their landmark 1978 book, *Gender: An Ethnomethodological Approach*, open the door to viewing gender as a social construct. They pinpoint various phenomena of gender, as follows:

Gender Assignment

Gender assignment happens when the culture says, "This is what you are." In most cultures, we're assigned a gender at birth. In our culture, once you've been assigned a gender, that's what you are; and for the most part, it's doctors who dole out the gender assignments, which shows you how emphatically gender has been medicalized. These doctors look down at a newly-born infant and say "It has a penis, it's a boy." Or they say, "It doesn't have a penis, it's a girl." It has little or nothing to do with vaginas. It's all penises or no penises: gender assignment is both phallocentric and genital. Other cultures are not or have not been so rigid.

In the early nineteenth century, Kodiak Islanders would occasionally assign a female gender to a child with a penis: this resulted in a woman who would bring great good luck to her husband, and a larger dowry to her parents. The European umbrella term for this and any other type of Native American transgendered person is *berdache*. Walter Williams in *The Spirit and the Flesh* chronicles nearly as many types of *berdache* as there were nations.

Even as early as 1702, a French explorer who lived for four years among the Illinois Indians noted that berdaches were known "from their childhood, when they are seen frequently picking up the spade, the spindle, the ax [women's tools], but making no use of the bow and arrow as all the other small boys do."

—Pierre Liette, Memoir of Pierre Liette on the Illinois Country

When the gender of a child was in question in some Navajo tribes, they reached a decision by putting a child inside a *tipi* with loom and a bow and arrow—female and male implements respectively. They set fire to the *tipi*, and whatever the child grabbed as he/she ran out determined the child's gender. It was perfectly natural to these Navajo that the child had some say in determining its own gender. Compare this method with the following modern example:

[The Montana Educational Telecommunica-
tions Network, a computer bulletin board,]
enabled students in tiny rural schools to communicate with students around the world.
Cynthia Denton, until last year a teacher at
the only public school in Hobson, Montana
(population 200), describes the benefit of
such links. "When we got our first messages
from Japan, a wonderful little fifth-grade girl
named Michelle was asked if she was a boy
or a girl. She was extraordinarily indignant at
that, and said, 'I'm Michelle—I'm a girl of
course.' Then I pointed out the name of the
person who had asked the question and said,
'Do you know if this is a boy or a girl?' She
said, 'No, how am I supposed to know that?'
I said, 'Oh, the rest of the world is supposed
to know that Michelle is a girl, but you have
no social responsibility to know if this is a boy
or a girl?' She stopped and said, 'Oh.' And
then she rephrased her reply considerably."
–Jacques Leslie, The Cursor Cowboy, 1993

Is the determination of one another's gender a "social responsibility?"

Do we have the legal or moral right to decide and assign our own genders?

Or does that right belong to the state, the church, and

the medical profession?

   If gender is classification, can we afford to throw away the very basic right to classify ourselves?

Gender Identity

Gender identity answers the question, "who am I?" Am I a man or a woman or a what? It's a decision made by nearly every individual, and it's subject to any influence: peer pressure, advertising, drugs, cultural definitions of gender, whatever.

   Gender identity is assumed by many to be "natural"; that is someone can feel "like a man," or "like a woman." When I first started giving talks about gender, this was the one question that would keep coming up: "Do you feel like a woman now?" "Did you ever feel like a man?" "How did you know what a woman would feel like?"

   I've no idea what "a woman" feels like. I never did feel like a girl or a woman; rather, it was my unshakable conviction that I was not a boy or a man. It was the absence of a feeling, rather than its presence, that convinced me to change my gender.

> What **does** a man feel like?
> What does a woman feel like?
> Do **you** feel "like a man?"
> Do you feel "like a woman?"
> I'd really like to know that from people.

Gender identity answers another question: "to which gender (class) do I want to belong?" Being and belonging are closely related concepts when it comes to gender. I felt I was a woman (being), and more importantly I felt I belonged with the other women (belonging). In this culture, the only two sanctioned gender clubs are "men" and "women." If you don't belong to one or the other, you're told in no uncertain terms to sign up fast.

Sweet Loretta Martin
Thought she was a woman

But she was another man.
All the girls around her
Thought she had it coming
But she gets it while she can.
Get back, get back,
Get back to where you once belonged.
Get back, Loretta.

    —John Lennon and Paul McCartney,
           Get Back, 1969

I remember a dream I had when I was no more than seven or eight years old—I might have been younger. In this dream, two lines of battle were drawn up facing one another on a devastated plain: I remember the earth was dry and cracked. An army of men on one side faced an army of women on the other. The soldiers on both sides were exhausted. They were all wearing skins—I remember smelling the un-tanned leather in my dream. I was a young boy, on the side of the men, and I was being tied down to a roughly-hewn cart. I wasn't struggling. When I was completely secured, the men attached a long rope to the cart, and tossed the other end of the rope over to the women. The soldiers of the women's army slowly pulled me across the empty ground between the two armies, as the sun began to rise. I could see only the sun and the sky. When I'd been pulled over to the side of the women, they untied me, turned their backs to the men, and we all walked away. I looked back, and saw the men walking away from us. We were all silent.

I wonder about reincarnation. I wonder how a child could have had a dream like that in such detail. I told this dream to the psychiatrist at the army induction center in Boston in 1969—they'd asked if I'd ever had any strange dreams, so I told them this one. They gave me a 1-Y, deferred duty due to psychiatric instability.

Gender Roles

Gender roles are collections of factors which answer the question, "How do I need to function so that society perceives me as belonging or not belonging to a specific gender?" Some people would include appearance, sexual orientation, and methods of communication under the term, but I think it makes more sense to think in terms of things like jobs, economic roles, chores, hobbies; in other words, positions and actions specific to a given gender as defined by a culture. Gender roles, when followed, send signals of membership in a given gender.

Gender Attribution

Then there's gender attribution, whereby we look at somebody and say, "that's a man," or "that's a woman." And this is important because the way we perceive another's gender affects the way we relate to that person. Gender attribution is the sneaky one. It's the one we do all the time without thinking about it; kinda like driving a sixteen-wheeler down a crowded highway…without thinking about it.

In this culture, gender attribution, like gender assignment, is phallocentric. That is, one is male until perceived otherwise. According to a study done by Kessler and McKenna, one can extrapolate that it would take the presence of roughly four female cues to outweigh the presence of one male cue: one is assumed male until proven otherwise. That's one reason why many women today get "sirred" whereas very few men get called "ma'am."

Gender attribution depends on cues given by the attributee, and perceived by the attributer. The categories of cues as I have looked at them apply to a man/woman bi-polar gender system, although they could be relevant to a more fluidly-gendered system. I found these cues to be useful in training actors in cross-gender role-playing.

Physical cues include body, hair, clothes, voice, skin, and movement.

> I'm nearly six feet tall, and I'm large-boned. Like most people born "male," my hands, feet, and forearms are proportionally larger to my body as a whole than those of

people born "female." My hair pattern included coarse facial hair. My voice is naturally deep—I sang bass in a high school choir and quartet. I've had to study ways and means of either changing these physical cues, or drawing attention away from them if I want to achieve a female attribution from people.

Susan Brownmiller's book, *Femininity*, is an excellent analysis of the social impact of physical factors as gender cues.

Behavioral cues include manners, decorum, protocol, and deportment. Like physical cues, behavioral cues change with time and culture. *Dear Abby* and other advice columnists often freely dispense gender-specific manners. Most of the behavioral cues I can think of boil down to how we occupy space, both alone and with others.

Some points of manners are not taught in books of etiquette. They are, instead, signals we learn from one another, mostly signals acknowledging membership to an upper (male) or lower (female) class. But to commit some of *these* manners in writing in terms of gender-specific behavior would be an acknowledgment that gender exists as a class system.

Here's one: As part of learning to pass as a woman, I was taught to avoid eye contact when walking down the street; that looking someone in the eye was a male cue. Nowadays, sometimes I'll look away, and sometimes I'll look someone in the eye—it's a behavior pattern that's more fun to play with than to follow rigidly. A femme cue (not "woman," but "femme") is to meet someone's eyes (usually a butch), glance quickly away, then slowly look back into the butch's eyes and hold that gaze: great, hot fun, that one!

In many transsexual and transvestite meetings I attended, when the subject of the discussion was "passing," a lot of emphasis was given to manners: who stands up to shake hands? who exits an elevator first? who opens doors? who lights cigarettes? These are all cues I had to learn in order to pass as a woman in this culture. It wasn't 'til I began to read feminist literature that I began to question these cues or to see them as oppressive.

Textual cues include histories, documents, names, associates, relationships—true or false—which support a desired gender attribution. Someone trying to be taken for male in this culture might take the name Bernard, which would probably get a better male attribution than the name Brenda.

Changing my name from Al to Kate was no big deal in Pennsylvania. It was a simple matter of filing a form with the court and publishing the name change in some unobtrusive "notices" column of a court-approved newspaper. Bingo—done. The problems came with changing all my documents. The driver's license was particularly interesting. Prior to my full gender change, I'd been pulled over once already dressed as a woman, yet holding my male driver's license—it wasn't something I cared to repeat.

Any changes in licenses had to be done in person at the Department of Motor Vehicles. I was working in corporate America: Ford Aerospace. On my lunch break, I went down to the DMV and waited in line with the other folks who had changes to make to their licenses. The male officer at the desk was flirting with me, and I didn't know what to do with that, so I kept looking away. When I finally got to the desk, he asked "Well young lady, what can we do for you?"

"I've got to make a name change on my license," I mumbled.

"Just get married?" he asked jovially.

"Uh, no," I replied.

"Oh! Divorced!" he proclaimed with just a bit of hope in his voice, "Let's see your license." I handed him my old driver's license with my male name on it. He glanced down at the card, apparently not registering what he saw. "You just go on over there, honey, and take your test. We'll have you fixed up soon. Oh," he added with a wink, "if you need anything special, you just come back here and ask old Fred."

I left old Fred and joined the line for my test. I handed the next officer both my license and my court order authorizing my name change. This time, the officer didn't give my license a cursory glance. He kept looking at me, then down at the paper, then me, then the paper. His face grim, he pointed over to the direction of the testing booths. On my way over to the booths, old Fred called out, "Honey, they treating you all right?" Before I could reply, the second officer snarled at old Fred to "get his butt over" to look at all my paperwork.

I reached the testing booths and looked back just in time to see a quite crestfallen old Fred looking at me, then the paper, then me, then the paper.

Mythic cues include cultural and sub-cultural myths which support membership in a given gender. This culture's myths include archetypes like: weaker sex, dumb blonde, strong silent type, and better half. Various waves of the women's movement have had to deal with a multitude of myths of male superiority.

Power dynamics as cue include modes of communication, communication techniques, and degrees of aggressiveness, assertiveness, persistence, and ambition.

Sexual orientation as cue highlights, in the dominant culture, the heterosexual imperative (or in the lesbian and gay culture, the homosexual imperative). For this reason, many male heterosexual transvestites who wish to pass as female will go out on a "date" with another man (who is dressed as a man)—the two seem to be a heterosexual couple. In glancing at the "woman" of the two, an inner dialogue might go, "It's wearing a dress, and it's hanging on the arm of a man, so it must be a woman."

For the same man to pass as a female in a lesbian bar, he'd need to be with a woman, dressed as a woman, as a "date."

> I remember one Fourth of July evening in Philadelphia, about a year after my surgery. I was walking home arm in arm with Lisa, my lover at the time, after the fireworks display. We were leaning in to one another, walking like lovers walk. Coming towards us was a family of five: mom, dad, and three teenage boys. "Look, it's a coupla faggots," said one of the boys. "Nah, it's two girls," said another. "That's enough outa you," bellowed the father, "one of 'em's got to be a man. This is America!"

So sex (the act) and gender (the classification) are different, and depending on the qualifier one is using for gender differentiation, they may or may not be dependent on one another. There are probably as many types of gender (gender systems) as could be imagined. Gender by clothing, gender by divine right, gender by lottery—these all make as much sense as any other criteria, but in our Western civilization, we bow down to the great god Science. No other type of gender holds as much sway as:

Biological gender, which classifies a person through any combination of body type, chromosomes, hormones, genitals, reproductive organs, or some other corporal or chemical essence. Belief in biological gender is in fact a belief in the supremacy of the body in the determination of identity. It's biological gender that most folks refer to when they say *sex*. By calling something "sex," we grant it seniority over all the other types of gender—by some right of biology.

So, there are all these *types* of gender which in and of themselves are *not* gender, but criteria for systemic classification. And there's sex, which somehow winds up on top of the heap. Add to this room full of seeds the words *male, female, masculine, feminine, man, woman, boy, girl*. These words are not descriptive of any sexual act, so all these words fall under the category of gender and are highly subjective, depending on which system of gender one is following.

But none of this explains why there is such a widespread insistence upon the conflation of *sex* and *gender*. I think a larger question is why Eurocentric culture needs to see *so much* in terms of sex.

It's not like gender is the **only** thing we confuse with sex. As a culture, we're encouraged to equate sex (the act) with money, success, and security; and with the products we're told will help us attain money, success and security. We live in a culture that succeeds in selling products (the apex of accomplishment in capitalism) by aligning those products with the attainment of one's sexual fantasies.

Switching my gender knocked me for a time curiously out of the loop of ads designed for men or women, gays or straights. I got to look at sex without the hype, and ads without the allure. None of them, after all, spoke to me, although all of them beckoned.

Kinds of Sex

"Can you orgasm with that vagina?"
—Audience member question for Kate
on the *Geraldo Rivera* show.

It's important to keep *gender* and *sex* separated as, respectively, *system* and *function*. Since function is easier to pin down than system, sex is a simpler starting place than gender.

"Yah, the plumbing works and so does the electricity."
—Kate's answer

There are so many sex manuals on the market—the how-to kind—and depending on where you look, there's bound to be one that talks about what you like to do. That's great, and I own several of them, but it's beyond the scope of this book. The purpose of talking about sex here is to disentangle it from gender.

Sex does have a primary factor to it which is germane to a discussion of gender: *sexual orientation*, which is what people call it, if they believe you're born with it, or *sexual preference* which is what people call it if they believe you have more of a choice and more of a say in the matter.

> [W]e do not need a sophisticated method-
> ology or technology to confirm that the
> gender component of identity is the most
> important one articulated during sex. Nearly
> everyone (except for bisexuals, perhaps)
> regards it as the prime criterion for choos-
> ing a sex partner.
>
> —Murray S. Davis, *Smut: Erotic*
> *Reality/Obscene Ideology,* 1983

The Basic Mix-Up

> A gay man who lived in Khartoum
> Took a lesbian up to his room.
> They argued all night
> Over who had the right
> To do what, and with what, to whom.
>
> —anonymous limerick

Here's the tangle that I found: sexual orientation/preference is based in this culture solely on the gender of one's partner of choice. Not only do we confuse the two words, we make them dependent on one another. The only choices we're given to determine the focus of our sexual desire are these:

>> *Heterosexual model:* in which a culturally-defined male is in a relationship with a culturally-defined female.
>> *Gay male model:* two culturally-defined men involved with each other.

>> *Lesbian model:* two culturally-defined women involved with each other.

>> *Bisexual model:* culturally-defined men and women who could be involved with either culturally-defined men or women.

Variants to these gender-based relationship dynamics would include heterosexual female with gay male, gay male with lesbian woman, lesbian woman with heterosexual woman, gay male with bisexual male, and so forth. People involved in these variants know that each dynamic is different from the other. A lesbian involved with another lesbian, for example, is a very different relationship than that of a lesbian involved with a bisexual woman, and *that's* distinct from being a lesbian woman involved with a heterosexual woman. What these variants have in common is that each of these combinations forms its own clearly-recognizable dynamic, and none of these are acknowledged by the dominant cultural binary of sexual orientation: heterosexuality/homosexuality.

Despite the non-recognition of these dynamics by the broader culture, *all these models depend on the gender of the partner.* This results in minimizing, if not completely dismissing, other dynamic models of a relationship which could be more important than gender and are often more telling about the real nature of someone's desire. There are so many factors on which we *could* base sexual orientation. Examples of alternate dynamic models include:

>> *Butch/Femme model,* however that may be defined by its participants.

Butch style, whether worn by men or women, is a symbol of detachment. Dressing butch gives the wearer the protection of being the observer, not the object. A femme-y look, by contrast, suggests self-display, whether in a quietly demure or sexually flashy fashion. Butch is a style of understatement: "I don't need to show flesh because I am in a position to choose. Butch

is no coy "come hither" look, but a chal-
lenge—"I see you and maybe I like what I
see."

There is something about femme-y style
that in itself produces insecurity, a sense of
vulnerability and exposure. The femme
invites the gaze and it takes a great deal of
feminine self-confidence to risk that kind of
scrutiny.

—Wendy Chapkis,
Beauty Secrets: Women and the Politics of
Appearance, 1986

>> *Top/Bottom model* which can be further sub-classified as domi-
nant/submissive or sadist/masochist.

The bottom is responsible for being obedi-
ent, for carrying out her top's orders with
dispatch and grace, for being as aroused and
sexually available and desirable as possible,
and for letting her top know when she is
physically uncomfortable or needs a
break....The top is responsible for con-
structing a scene that falls within the
bottom's limits, although it is permissible
to stretch her limit if she suddenly discov-
ers the capacity to go further than she ever
has before.

—Pat Califia, *Sapphistry: The Book of*
Lesbian Sexuality, 1983

There are also:

Butch/Butch models
Femme/Femme models
Triad (or more) models
Human/Animal models

Adult/Child models
Same-aged models
Parent/Child models
Multiple partners models
Able-bodied models
Differently-abled bodies models
Reproductive models
Owner/Slave models
Monogamous models
Non-monogamous models

I'm sure I'm leaving models out of this, and someone is going to be really upset that I didn't think of them, but the point is there's more to sex (the act) than gender (one classification of identity).

> Try making a list of ways in which sexual preference or orientation could be measured, and then add to that list (or subtract from it) every day for a month, or a year (or for the rest of your life). Could be fun!

Sex Without Gender

There are plenty of instances in which sexual attraction can have absolutely nothing to do with the gender of one's partner.

When Batman and Catwoman try to get it on sexually, it only works when they are both in their caped crusader outfits. Naked heterosexuality is a miserable failure between them....When they encounter each other in costume however something much sexier happens and the only thing missing is a really good scene where we get to hear the delicious sound of Catwoman's latex rubbing on Batman's black rubber/leather skin. To me their

*flirtation in capes looked queer precisely
because it was not heterosexual, they
were not man and woman, they were bat
and cat, or latex and rubber, or feminist
and vigilante: gender became irrelevant
and sexuality was dependent on many
other factors....*

*You could also read their sexual encoun-
ters as the kind of sex play between gay
men and lesbians that we are hearing so
much about recently: in other words, the
sexual encounter is queer because both
partners are queer and the genders of
the participants are less relevant. Just
because Batman is male and Catwoman is
female does not make their interactions
heterosexual—think about it, there is
nothing straight about two people getting
it on in rubber and latex costumes, wearing eyemasks and carrying whips and other
accoutrements.*

—Judith Halberstam, "Queer
Creatures," *On Our Backs,*
Nov/Dec, 1992

Sexual preference *could* be based on genital preference. (This is not the
same as saying preference for a specific gender, unless you're basing
your definition of gender on the presence or absence of some combination of genitals.) Preference could also be based on the kind of sex *acts*
one prefers, and, in fact, elaborate systems exist to distinguish just that,
and to announce it to the world at large. For example, here's a handkerchief code from the Samois Collective's *Coming To Power.* The code is
used for displaying preference in sexual behavior. Colors mean active
if worn on the left side, or passive if worn on the right.

Left Side	Color	Right Side
Fist Fucker	Red	Fist Fuckee
Anal Sex, Top	Dark Blue	Anal Sex, Bottom
Oral Sex, Top	Light Blue	Oral Sex, Bottom
Light S/M, Top	Robin's Egg Blue	Light S/M, Bottom
Foot Fetish, Top	Mustard	Foot Fetish, Bottom
Anything Goes, Top	Orange	Anything Goes, Bottom
Gives Golden Showers	Yellow	Wants Golden Showers
Hustler, Selling	Green	Hustler, Buying
Uniforms/Military, Top	Olive Drab	Uniforms/Military, Bottom
Likes Novices, Chickenhawk	White	Novice (or Virgin)
Victorian Scenes	White Lace	Victorian Scenes, Bottom
Does Bondage	Grey	Wants to be put in Bondage
Shit Scenes, Top	Brown	Shit Scenes, Bottom
Heavy S/M & Whipping, Top	Black	Heavy S/M & Whipping, Bottom
Piercer	Purple	Piercee
Likes Menstruating Women	Maroon	Is Menstruating
Group Sex, Top	Lavender	Group Sex, Bottom
Breast Fondler	Pink	Breast Fondlee

I love this code! It gave me quite a few ideas when I first read it. But despite the many variations possible, sexual orientation/preference remains culturally linked to our gender system (and by extension to gender identity) through the fact that it's most usually based on the gender of one's partner. This link probably accounts for much of the tangle between sex and gender.

The confusion between sex and gender affects more than individuals and relationships. The conflation of sex and gender contributes to the linking together of the very different subcultures of gays, lesbians, bisexuals, leather sexers, sex-workers, and the transgendered.

A common misconception is that male cross-dressers are both gay and prostitutes, whereas the truth of the matter is that most cross-dressers that I've met hold down more mainstream jobs, careers, or professions, are married, and are practicing heterosexuals.

A dominant culture tends to combine its subcultures into manageable units. As a result, those who practice non-traditional sex are seen by members of the dominant culture (as well as by members of sex and gender subcultures) as a whole with those who don non-traditional gender roles and identities. Any work to deconstruct the gender system needs to take into account the artificial amalgam of subcultures, which might itself collapse if the confusion of terms holding it together were to be settled.

In any case, if we buy into categories of sexual orientation based solely on gender—heterosexual, homosexual, or bisexual—we're cheating ourselves of a searching examination of our real sexual preferences. In the same fashion, by subscribing to the categories of gender based solely on the male/female binary, we cheat ourselves of a searching examination of our real gender identity. And now we can park sex off to the side for a while, and bring this essay back around to gender.

Desire

I was not an unattractive man. People's reactions to my gender change often included the remonstrative, "But you're such a good-looking guy!" Nowadays, as I navigate the waters between male and female, there are still people attracted to me. At first, my reaction was fear: "What kind of pervert," I thought, "would be attracted to a freak like me?" As I got over that internalized phobia of my transgender status, I began to get curious about the nature of desire, sex, and identity. When, for example, I talk about the need to do away with gender, I always get looks of horror from the audience: "What about desire and attraction!" they want to know, "How can you have desire with no gender?" They've got a good point: the concepts of sex and gender seem to overlap around the phenomenon of desire. So I began to explore my transgendered relationship to desire.

> About five months into living full-time as a woman, I woke up one morning and felt really good about the day. I got dressed for work, and checking the mirror before I left, I liked what I saw—at last! I opened the door to

leave the building, only to find two workmen standing on
the porch, the hand of one poised to knock on the door.
This workman's face lit up when he saw me. "Well!" he
said, "Don't you look beautiful today." At that moment, I
realized I didn't know how to respond to that. I felt like a
deer caught in the headlights of an oncoming truck. I
really wasn't prepared for people to be attracted to me.
To this day, I don't know how to respond to a man who's
attracted to me—I never learned the rituals.

To me, desire is a wish to experience someone or something that I've
never experienced, or that I'm not currently experiencing. Usually, I
need an identity appropriate (or appropriately inappropriate) to the
context in which I want to experience that person or thing. This context could be anything: a romantic involvement, a tennis match, or a
boat trip up a canal. On a boat trip up the canal, I could appropriately
be a passenger or a crew member. In a tennis match, I could be a player,
an audience member, a concessionaire, a referee, a member of the
grounds staff. In the context of a romantic involvement, it gets less obvious about what I need to be in order to have an appropriate identity, but
I would need to have *some* identity. Given that most romantic or sexual
involvements in this culture are defined by the genders of the partners,
the *most* appropriate identity to have in a romantic relationship would
be a gender identity, or something that passes for gender identity, like a
gender role. A gender role might be butch, femme, top, and bottom—
these are all methods of acting. So, even without a gender identity *per se*,
some workable identity can be called up and put into motion within a
relationship, and when we play with our identities, we play with desire.
Some identities stimulate desire, others diminish desire. To make ourselves attractive to someone, we modify our identity, or at least the
appearance of an identity—and this includes gender identity.

I love the idea of being without an identity, it gives me a lot of room
to play around; but it makes me dizzy, having nowhere to hang my hat.
When I get too tired of not having an identity, I take one on: it doesn't
really matter what identity I take on, as long as it's recognizable. I can
be a writer, a lover, a confidante, a femme, a top, or a woman. I retreat

into definition as a way of demarcating my space, a way of saying "Step back, I'm getting crowded here." By saying "I am the (fill in the blank)," I also say, "You are *not*, and so you are not in my space." Thus, I achieve privacy. Gender identity is a form of self-definition: something into which we can withdraw, from which we can glean a degree of privacy from time to time, and with which we can, to a limited degree, manipulate desire.

Our culture is obsessed with desire: it drives our economy. We come right out and say we're going to stimulate desire for goods and services, and so we're bombarded daily with ads and commercial announcements geared to make us desire things. No wonder the emphasis on desire spills over into the rest of our lives. No wonder I get panicked reactions from audiences when I suggest we eliminate gender as a system; gender defines our desire, and we don't know what to do if we don't have desire. Perhaps the more importance a culture places on desire, the more conflated become the concepts of sex and gender.

As an exercise, can you recall the last time you saw someone whose gender was ambiguous? Was this person attractive to you? And if you knew they called themselves neither a man nor a woman, what would it make you if you're attracted to that person? And if you were to kiss? Make love? What would you be?

> I remember one time at a gay and lesbian writers' conference in San Francisco, I was on a panel and asking these same questions. Because it was a specifically gay and lesbian audience, an audience that defined itself by its sexual orientation, I wanted to tweak them on that identity. I asked, "And what if I strapped on a dildo and made love to you: what would that make me?" Without missing a beat, panelist Carol Queen piped up, "Nostalgic."

<< 5 >>

INTERLUDE
The Lesbian Thing

Issues: *The thing that really fascinates me is that as a man, you were heterosexual, in the eyes of the construct, anyway. Did you feel like you were a man who was a lesbian?*

Kate: I didn't feel like I was a man. Ever. I was *being* a man, but I never felt like I was. I was, in every aspect, fulfilling the gender role of "man." The societal role of man. And so socially, I was a man. No question. But I never *felt* like I was.

Justin: *What is the difference between the way that heterosexual women related to you, and the way that lesbians relate to you now?*

Kate: Real good question! When I was being a man relating with a woman, there was much more of an assumed "man role" and an assumed "woman role," and it was dichotomized. For the most part, there were certain constructs that were assumed, patterns of relating that are uniquely heterosexual that would be silly to try now. Now there's much more negotiating, much more talking, and much more fluidity in terms of roles in relating with women. Also, there's a distance in a heterosexual relationship. There can be a certain kind of getting together, but then there's always,

"What the fuck *are* you anyway?" It stops, it just stops. And in a lesbian relationship—and I'm assuming it's the same in a homosexual male relationship, I don't know—there's much more familiarity. There's just much more closeness.

Issues: *Were you ever attracted to men?*

Kate: I had fantasies about men. But was I ever attracted to a man? One [looks at Justin—they smile]. That was a crush, and I just couldn't understand it. "What is this?!" I was just hopelessly crushed out on Justin. And it was so intriguing. I've gotten over that to the point where I just love him so dearly, I just feel really close to him. But beyond that, no. I was never attracted to a man. I've had sex with men, prior to my surgery, and certainly not afterwards, and did not enjoy it. I still have fantasies, though, and they're fun, and sometimes during sex, my girlfriend and I would take turns strapping on dildos—which isn't the same as being a man or playing at being a man—and I'd look down at this thing and say "Oh, I remember *that!*" [lots of laughter all around]. My lover says I'm more practiced than any of her other women lovers. It's lots of fun [laughter].

Acceptance in the Lesbian Community

Taste Of Latex: *What's the reaction in the lesbian community to your being a transsexual lesbian? Were you seeking acceptance, and did you find it?*

Kate: I sought acceptance in one lesbian community that had a bad experience with a transsexual lesbian five or six years prior to my being there. According to women who were there, she had attempted a power play to take over this huge lesbian organization in the city, and the reaction was very strong, very vocal. The reaction was very much, "Well that's a man for you!"

Then I came along, and they were like "LOOK-OUT, another one!" People wouldn't know I was a transsexual and then they'd find out and they'd be like "Oh, I knew all along: it was male energy, I felt that!" It was not very good acceptance. I [did find] acceptance with people much younger than me. People in their twenties and thirties were much more accepting than my generation who are major fuddy-duds.

Now, it doesn't matter that much. I don't hang where I'm not accepted. I still get some people who have problems, who say "Well, you're not really a woman," and I say, "Right..." And they say, "Well, how can you be a lesbian?" and to me that's the heart of it—I try to engage those folks by asking, "What's a woman? What's a man?" I wish someone would answer me that—it would make my life a lot easier. I could get on playing some other kind of game. But no one has been able to answer that. There's no hard and fast rule.

But there are rules. And there is a rulebook.

Asbury Park Public School photo, about ten years old.

« 6 »

ABANDON YOUR TEDIOUS SEARCH

The Rulebook Has Been Found!

In the '80s, there were a lot of theories about addiction and co-dependence. Most of these agreed on the point that we get addicted to some thing in order to avoid or deny some other thing. Workaholics work, alcoholics drink, and sexaholics fuck. I look at gender in the same light: it's something we do to avoid or deny our full self-expression. People, I believe, compulsively act out gender—there actually are rules on how to do this.

I'd better not go too far on this, or someone will start a twelve-step program around this idea! Nonetheless, there **are** rules of gender.

The rules of gender are termed the "natural attitude" of our culture (the real, objective facts) per Harold Garfinkel's 1967 *Studies in Ethnomethodology*. I like to read these rules every now and then to see how each rule has continued to play a part in my life—it's frighteningly accurate. I keep in touch with these rules—it helps me figure out new ways of breaking them. Here are Mr. Garfinkle's rules, and a few ideas about each*:

*Garfinkle, Harold, *Studies in Ethnomethodology.* Englewood Cliffs, N.J.: Prentice-Hall, 1967.

1. There are two, and only two, genders (female and male).

The first question we usually ask new parents is: Is it a boy or a girl?
There's a great answer to that one going around: "We don't know; it
hasn't told us yet." Personally, I think no question containing *either/or*
deserves a serious answer, and that includes the question of gender.

> I'm a member of a commercial electronic bulletin board
> service called **America Online**. My screen name is
> **OutlawGal**. I inevitably get two queries: "What
> makes you an outlaw?" to which I always reply that I
> break the laws of nature. The second question is almost
> always, "M or F?" to which I answer, "Yes." Anyone who
> has a sense of humor about that is someone I want to
> keep talking with.

2. One's gender is invariant. (If you are female/male, you always were female/male and you always will be female/male.)

> *The latest transsexual notable has been
> Renee Richards who has succeeded in hitting
> the benefits of sex discrimination back into
> the male half of the court. The public recog-
> nition and success that it took Billie Jean
> King and women's tennis years to get, Renee
> Richards has achieved in one set. The new
> bumper stickers might well read: "It takes
> castrated balls to play women's tennis."*
>   —Janice G. Raymond,
>   *The Transexual Empire*, 1979

Despite her vicious attack on transsexuals, Raymond's book is a worth-
while read, chiefly for its intelligent highlighting of the male-dominated
medical profession, and that profession's control of transsexual surgery.
Raymond and her followers believe in some essential thing called
"woman," and some other essential thing called "man," and she sees

transgendered people as encroaching in her space. Raymond obeys the rules: in her world view, there can be no mutable gender.

> There have been both cultural feminists and hard-line fundamentalists who have agreed that I was not only born male, but that no matter what happened to me, and no matter my choices, I will remain male 'til the day I die. I no longer dispute people like that: that's how they're going to experience me no matter what I say or do. As long as they neither threaten me nor keep me from entering any public space, I feel more sorry for them than anything else.

3. **Genitals are the essential sign of gender. (A female is a person with a vagina; a male is a person with a penis.)**

> I never hated my penis; I hated that it made me a man—in my own eyes, and in the eyes of others. For my comfort, I needed a vagina—I was convinced that the only way I could live out what I thought to be my true gender was to have genital surgery to construct a vagina from my penis. Fortunately, I don't regret having done this.
>
> It's real interesting all the papers you have to sign before actually getting male-to-female gender reassignment surgery. I had to acknowledge the possibility of every surgical mishap: from never having any sensation in my genitals, to never having another orgasm in my life, to the threat of my newly-constructed labia falling off. As it turned out, I have some slight loss of feeling on the surface of the skin around my vagina, but I can achieve orgasms, and the last time I looked my labia were still in place. Like I said, I'm lucky; some folks aren't.

4. **Any exceptions to two genders are not to be taken seriously. (They must be jokes, pathology, etc.)**

I remember one time walking into a Woolworth's in Philadelphia. I'd been living as a woman for about a month. I came through the revolving doors, and stood face to face with a security guard—a young man, maybe nineteen or twenty years old. He did a double take when he saw me and he began to laugh—very loud. He just laughed and laughed. I continued round through the revolving doors and left the store. I agreed with him that I was a joke; that I was the sick one.

I went back in there almost a year later. He came on to me.

5. **There are no transfers from one gender to another except ceremonial ones (masquerades).**

The Mummers' Parade is held annually on New Year's Day in Philadelphia. Hundreds of men—mostly blue-collar family men—dress up in sequins, feathers, and gowns, and parade up and down the main streets of the City of Brotherly Love.

In most shamanic cultures, there exists a ceremonial rite whereby spiritual leaders , like the Siberian "soft man," need to live part of their lives as another gender before attaining the rank of spiritual leader.

The transformation [from man to "soft man"] takes place gradually when the boy is between ages eight and fifteen, the critical years when shamanistic inspiration usually manifests itself. The Chukshi feel that this transformation is due to powerful spirits.
—Walter L. Williams, *The Spirit and the Flesh*, 1986

6. **Everyone must be classified as a member of one gender or another. (There are no cases where gender is not attributed.)**

> Do you know anyone to whom you've not assigned the gender male or the gender female? Isn't that a hoot? That alone makes it important for each of us to question gender's grip on our society.

7. **The male/female dichotomy is a "natural" one. (Males and females exist independently of scientists' [or anyone else's] criteria for being male or female.)**

There is black on one side of a spectrum, and

                                                white

                                      on the other

          with a middle ground of grey, or

     some would say there's a rainbow between the two.

There is

left, and

                                            right

          and a middle ground of center.

There is birth on one side,

                        and death on the other side

          and a middle ground of life.

Yet we insist that there are two,   And we insist that this

only two genders: male and female.   is the way of nature.

Blue

                                        yellow

                 green.

Nature?

                                  Nature?

              Nature.

8. **Membership in one gender or another is "natural." (Being
    female or male is not dependent on anyone's deciding what
    you are.)**

In the mid-80s, when I first got involved with women's
politics, and gay and lesbian politics, I saw these buttons
that read:

KEEP YOUR LAWS
OFF
MY BODY!

or

BIOLOGY
IS NOT
DESTINY!

I thought they were particularly relevant to my situation
as a transsexual. But I found out otherwise. If I attempt
to decide my own gender, I am apparently transgressing
against nature—never mind what the buttons said.

When I entered the women's community in the mid-80s,
I was told that I still had male energy. (I never knew what
"male energy" was, but I later figured out that it was the
last of my male privilege showing.) They said that I'd been
socialized as a male, and could never truly be a female;
that what I was, in fact, was a castrated male. And that
hurt me for a long time—over a year, in fact.

I kept hearing people define me in terms *they* were comfortable with. It's
easy to play victim, and to say that these people were being malicious,
but assuming the worst about others is simply not truth, and it's not a
loving or empowering way to look at other people. So, I began to look at
their investment in defining me. What I found was that each person who

was anxious to define me had a stake in maintaining his or her own membership in a given gender. I began to respect the needs of those who had a stake in their genders.

So I began to say things like, "Yep, I'm a castrated man all right, if that's what you see." And my joy at the look on their faces was the beginning of my sense of humor about all of this—I was no longer humiliated by their definitions of me.

I still have my

KEEP YOUR LAWS
OFF
MY BODY!

button—it's more nostalgic than anything else.

Somewhere, Beyond the Rules

So there are rules to gender, but rules can be broken. On to the next secret of gender—gender can have ambiguity. There are many ways to transgress a prescribed gender code, depending upon the world view of the person who's doing the transgressing: they range from preferring to be somewhat less than rigidly-gendered, to preferring an entirely non-definable image. Achievement of these goals ranges from doing nothing, to maintaining several wardrobes, to full surgical transformation.

It doesn't really matter what a person decides to do, or how radically a person plays with gender. What matters, I think, is how aware a person is of the options. How sad for a person to be missing out on some expression of identity, just for not knowing there are options.

And then I found out that gender can have fluidity, which is quite different from ambiguity. If ambiguity is a refusal to fall within a prescribed gender code, then fluidity is the refusal to remain one gender or another. Gender fluidity is the ability to freely and knowingly become one or many of a limitless number of genders, for any length of time, at any rate of change. Gender fluidity recognizes no borders or rules of gender.

> A fluid identity, incidentally, is one way to solve problems with boundaries. As a person's identity keeps shifting, so do individual borders and boundaries. It's hard to cross a boundary that keeps moving!

It was the discovery of my own ambiguity and fluidity of gender that led me to my gender change. It was figuring out these two concepts that allowed me to observe these factors—inhibited or in full bloom—in the culture, and in individuals.

At home in New Jersey, age 13 or 14. I'd already learned to smile for a camera, no matter what was going on.

claiming power

I learned from working in the Women's Movement that one of the first steps in claiming power is to speak one's own voice: to name oneself. Having sorted out the culture's ideas of gender and sexuality, it's time to name the experience of stepping outside those ideas.

*Launcelot Gobbo, the clown in Shakespeare's **The Merchant of Venice**, at Faunce House Theater, Brown University, 1966, directed by Janice Van der Water Brown.*

« 7 »

WHICH OUTLAWS?
or, Who Was That Masked Man?

On the day of my birth, my grandparents gave me a television set. In 1948, this was a new and wonderful thing. It had a nine-inch screen embedded in a cherrywood case the size of my mother's large oven.

My parents gave over an entire room to the television set. It was "the television room."

I've tried to figure out which questions get to the core of transgender issues—the answer to the riddle of my oddly-gendered life would probably be found in the area we question the least, and there are many areas of gender we do not question. We talk casually, for example, about *trans*-gender without ever clearly stating, and rarely if ever asking, what one gender or the other really is. We're so sure of our ability to categorize people as either men or women that we neglect to ask ourselves some very basic questions: what is a man? and what is a woman? and why do we need to be one or the other?

If we ask by what criteria a person might classify someone as being either male or female, the answers appear to be so self-evident as to make the question trivial. But consider a list of items that differentiate

*females from males. There are none that
always and without exception are true of
only one gender.*
    —Kessler and McKenna, *Gender: An
    Ethnomethodological Approach,* 1976

Touching All the Basis

Most folks would define a man by the presence of a penis or some form
of a penis. Some would define a woman by the presence of a vagina or
some form of a vagina. It's not that simple, though. I know several
women in San Francisco who have penises. Many wonderful men in my
life have vaginas. And there are quite a few people whose genitals fall
somewhere between penises and vaginas. What are *they?*

Are you a man because you have an *XY* chromosome? A woman
because you have *XX?* Unless you're an athlete who's been challenged
in the area of gender representation, you probably haven't had a chromosome test to determine your gender. If you haven't had that test, then
how do you know what gender you are, and how do you know what
gender your romantic or sexual partner is? There are, in addition to the
XX and *XY* pairs, some other commonly-occurring sets of gender chromosomes, including *XXY, XXX, YYY, XYY,* and *XO.* Does this mean
there are more than two genders?

Let's keep looking. What makes a man—testosterone? What makes a
woman—estrogen? If so, you could buy your gender over the counter at
any pharmacy. But we're taught that there are these things called "male"
and "female" hormones; and that testosterone dominates the gender
hormone balance in the males of any species. Not really—female hye-
nas, for example, have naturally more testosterone than the males; the
female clitoris resembles a very long penis—the females mount the
males from the rear, and proceed to hump. While some female humans I
know behave in much the same manner as the female hyena, the example demonstrates that the universal key to gender is not hormones.

Are you a woman because you can bear children? Because you bleed
every month? Many women are born without this potential, and every
woman ceases to possess that capability after menopause—do these

women cease being women? Does a necessary hysterectomy equal a gender change?

Are you a man because you can father children? What if your sperm count is too low? What if you were exposed to nuclear radiation and were rendered sterile? Are you then a woman?

Are you a woman because your birth certificate says female? A man because your birth certificate says male? If so, how did *that* happen? A doctor looked down at your crotch at birth. A doctor decided, based on what was showing of your external genitals, that you would be one gender or another. You never had a say in that most irreversible of all pronouncements—and according to this culture as it stands today, you never *will* have a say. What if you had been born a hermaphrodite, with some combination of both genitals? A surgeon would have "fixed" you—without your consent, and possibly without the consent or even knowledge of your parents, depending on your race and economic status. You would have been fixed—fixed into a gender. It's a fairly common experience being born with different or anomalous genitals, but we don't allow hermaphrodites in modern Western medicine. We "fix" them.

But let's get back to that birth certificate. Are you female or male because of what the law says? Is law immutable? Aren't we legislating every day in order to change the laws of our state, our nation, our culture? Isn't that the name of the game when it comes to political progress? What about other laws—religious laws, for example. Religions may dictate right and proper behavior for men and women, but no religion actually lays out what is a man and what is a woman. They assume we know, that's how deep this cultural assumption runs.

I've been searching all my life for a rock-bottom definition of woman, an unquestionable sense of what is a man. I've found nothing except the fickle definitions of gender held up by groups and individuals for their own purposes.

Every day I watched it, that television told me what was a man and what was a woman.

And every day I watched it, that television told me what to buy in order to be a woman.

And everything I bought, I said to myself I am a real
woman, and I never once admitted that I was transsexual.
You could say I'm one inevitability of a post-modern anti-
spiritualist acquisitive culture.

A Question of Priorities

I haven't found any answers. I ask every day of my life what is a man
and what is a woman, and those questions beg the next: why? Why do
we have to be one or the other? Why do we have to be gendered creatures at all? What keeps the bi-polar gender system in place?

I started out thinking that a theory of gender would bridge the long-
standing gap between the two major genders, male and female. I'm no
longer trying to do that. Some people think I want a world without gender, something bland and colorless: that's so far from how I live! I love
playing with genders, and I love watching other people play with all the
shades and flavors that gender can come in. I just want to question what
we've been holding on to for such an awfully long time. I want to question the existence of gender, and I want to enter that question firmly
into the fabric of this culture.

I used to watch **The Lone Ranger** on television. I loved
that show. This masked guy rides into town on a white
horse, does all these great and heroic deeds, everyone falls
in love with him and then he leaves. He never takes off his
mask, no one ever sees his face. He leaves behind a silver
bullet and the memory of someone who can do no wrong.
No bad rumors, no feet of clay, no cellulite. What a life!
There's a self-help book in there somewhere. **Who Was
That Masked Man? Learning to Overcome
the Lone Ranger Syndrome**.

As I moved through the '50s and '60s, I bought into the fear and hatred
that marks this culture's attitude toward the genderless and the non-
traditionally gendered. People are genuinely afraid of being without a
gender. I've been chewing on that fear nearly all my life like it was some

old bone, and now I want to take that fear apart to see what makes it tick. Nothing in the culture has encouraged me to stay and confront that fear. Instead, the culture has kept pointing me toward one door or the other:

Girls or Boys
Men or Women
Ladies or Gentlemen
Cats or Chicks
Faggots or Dykes

I knew from age four on, that something was wrong with me being a guy, and I spent most of my life avoiding the issue of my transsexuality. I hid out in textbooks, pulp fiction, and drugs and alcohol. I numbed my mind with everything from peyote to Scientology. I buried my head in the sands of television, college, a lot of lovers, and three marriages. Because I was being raised as a male, I never got to experience what it meant to be raised female in this culture. All I had were my observations, and all I could observe and assimilate as a child were differences in clothing and manners. I remember building a catalogue of gestures, phrases, body language, and outfits in my head. I would practice all of these at night when my parents had gone to sleep. I'd wear a blanket as a dress, and I'd stand in front of my mirror being my latest crush at school—I was so ashamed of myself for that.

> I was obsessed, and like most obsessed people, I was the last one to know it. The culture itself is obsessed with gender—and true to form, the culture as a whole will be the last to find out how obsessed it really has been.

Why We Haven't Asked Questions

I know there must have been other kids—boys and girls—going through the same remorse-filled hell that held me prisoner in front of my bedroom mirror, but we had no way of knowing that: there was no language for what we were doing. Instead, cardboard cut-out versions of us were creeping into the arts and media: in poetry, drama, dance, music, sculpture, paintings, television, cinema—in just about any art form you can think of there have been portrayals of people who are ambiguously or differently-gendered, all drawn by people who were not us, all spoken in voices that were not ours.

> Dominant cultures tend to colonize and control minorities through stereotyping—it's no different with the trans- gender minority. Make us a joke and there's no risk of our anger, no fear we'll raise some unified voice in protest, because we're not organized. But that's changing.

We never did fit into the cultural binary of male/female, man/woman, boy/girl. No, we are the clowns, the sex objects, or the mysteriously unattainable in any number of novels. We are the psychotics, the mur- derers, or the criminal geniuses who populate the movies. Audiences have rarely seen the real faces of the transgendered. They don't hear our voices, rarely read our words. For too many years, we transgendered people have been playing a hiding game, appearing in town one day, wearing a mask, and leaving when discovery was imminent. We would never tell anyone who we were, and so we were never really able to find one another. That's just now beginning to change.

> See, when we walk into a restaurant and we see another transsexual person, we look the other way, we pretend we don't exist. There's no sly smile, no secret wink, signal, or handshake. Not yet. We still quake in solitude at the prospect of recognition, even if that solitude is in the company of our own kind.

Silence=Death

—ACT-UP slogan

Silence of the Meek-as-Lambs

Simply saying "Come out, come out, wherever you are," is not going to bring the multitudes of transgendered people out into the open. Before saying that coming out is an option (and I believe it's an inevitable step, one we're all going to have to take at some time), it's necessary to get transgendered people talking with one another. The first step in coming out in the world is to come out to our own kind.

Before I dealt with my gender change, I had gold card membership in the dominant culture. To all appearances, I was a straight, white, able-bodied, middle-class male. I fought so hard against being transsexual because I heard all the teasing and jokes in the locker rooms. I saw people shudder or giggle when they'd talk about Renee Richards or Christine Jorgensen. I was all too aware of the disgust people were going through when *Playboy* published its interview with Wendy Carlos. I watched Caroline Cossey (Tula) get dragged through the mud of the press on two continents. The lesson was there time after time. Of course we were silent.

In the summer of 1969, I drove across Canada and the United States, living out of my Volkswagen station wagon that I'd named Mad John after my acting teacher. I was a hippie boy, hair down past my shoulders and dressed very colorfully: beads, headband, bellbottoms. I pulled into a state park in South Dakota to camp for the night. Some good ol' boys came up to my campsite and began the usual "Hey, girl" comments. I ignored them, and they eventually went away. Later that night, I woke up in my sleeping bag with a hand on my chest and a knife in front of my face. "Maybe we wanna fuck you, girl," is what this guy said. He brought the knife down to my face—I could feel how cold and sharp it was. "Maybe you oughta get outa here before we fuck you and beat the shit outa you." Then I was alone in the dark with only the sound of the wind in the trees. I packed up camp and left.

The following summer, I traveled across country again, this time in a VW mini-bus, but I stuck to more populated areas: I'd learned. Too many transgendered people don't get off that easy.

What a Tangled Web We Weave...

A less visible reason for the silence of the transgendered hinges on the fact that transsexuality in this culture is considered an illness, and an illness that can only be cured by silence.

Here's how this one works: we're taught that we are literally sick, that we have an illness that can be diagnosed and maybe cured. As a result of the medicalization of our condition, transsexuals must see therapists in order to receive the medical seal of approval required to proceed with any gender reassignment surgery. Now, once we get to the doctor, we're told we'll be cured if we become members of one gender or another. We're told not to divulge our transsexual status, except in select cases requiring intimacy. Isn't that amazing? Transsexuals presenting themselves for therapy in this culture are channeled through a system which labels them as having a disease (transsexuality) for which the therapy is to lie, hide, or otherwise remain silent.

> I was told by several counselors and a number of transgendered peers that I would need to invent a past for myself as a little girl, that I'd have to make up incidents of my girl childhood; that I'd have to say things like "When I was a little girl...." I never was a little girl; I'd lied all my life trying to be the boy, the man that I'd known myself **not** to be. Here I was, taking a giant step toward personal integrity by entering therapy with the truth and self-acknowledgment that I was a transsexual, and I was told, "Don't **tell** anyone you're transsexual."

Transsexuality is the only condition for which the therapy is to lie. This therapeutic lie is one reason we haven't been saying too much about ourselves and our lives and our experience of gender; we're not allowed, in therapy, the right to think of ourselves as transsexual.

This was where a different kind of therapy might have helped me. Perhaps if I hadn't spent so much time thinking and talking about being a woman, and perhaps if the

psychiatrist who examined me had spent
less time focusing on those aspects of my
life which could never be changed by surgery,
I would have had more opportunity to think
about myself as a transsexual. It was expo-
sure to the press that forced me to talk
about my transsexuality, and it was a painful
way to have to learn to do so.
    —Caroline Cossey, *My Story*, 1992

Another reason for the silence of transsexuals is the mythology of the transgender subculture. Two or more transsexuals together, goes the myth, can be read more easily *as* transsexual—so they don't pass. I don't think that's it.

I think transsexuals keep away from each other because we threaten the hell out of one another.

Each of us, transsexual and non-transsexual, develop a view of the world as we grow up—a view that validates our existence, gives us a reason for being, a justification for the nuttinesses that each of us might have. Most non-transsexuals have cultural norms on which to pin their world view, broadcast by magazines, television, cinema, electronic bulletin boards, and the continually growing list of communications environments.

Since transsexuals in this culture are neither fairly nor accurately represented in the media, nor championed by a community, we develop our world views in solitude. Alone, we figure out why we're in the world the way we are. The literature to date on the transgender experience does not help us to establish a truly transgender world view in concert with other transgender people, because virtually all the books and theories about gender and transsexuality to date have been written by non-transsexuals who, no matter how well-intentioned, are each trying to figure out how to make us fit into *their* world view. Transgendered people learn to explain gender to themselves from a very early age.

When I was ten or eleven years old, I used to play alone in the basement, way back in the corner where no one would come along to disturb me. There was an old chair there to which I attached all manner of wires and boxes and dials: it was my gender-change machine. I would sit in that chair and twist the dials, and—presto—I was off on an adventure in my mind as a little girl, usually some budding dykelet like Nancy Drew or Pippi Longstocking.

Most transsexuals opt for the theory that there are men and women and no in-between ground: the agreed-upon gender system. That's what I did—I just knew I had to be one or the other—so, in my world view, I saw myself as a mistake: some*thing* that needed to be fixed and then placed neatly into one of the categories.

There are some wonderfully subtle differences in the world views developed by individual transsexuals. Talk to a few transgendered people and see how beautifully textured the normally drab concept of gender can become.

We bring our very personal explanations for our existence into contact with other transsexuals who have been spending *their* lives constructing their *own* reasons for existence. If, when we meet, our world views differ radically enough, we wind up threatening each other's basic understanding of the world—we threaten each other. So we'd rather not meet, we'd rather not talk. At this writing, that's starting to change. Transsexuals and other transgendered people are finally sitting down, taking stock, comparing notes—and it's the dominant culture that's coming up short. Some of us are beginning to actually like ourselves and each other for the blend we are. Many of us are beginning to express our discontent with a culture that wants us silent.

This Western culture of ours tends to sacrifice the full range of experience to a lower common denominator that's acceptable to more people; we end up with

McDonald's instead of real food, Holiday Inns instead of homes, and **USA Today** instead of news and cultural analysis. And we do that with the rest of our lives.

Our spirits are full of possibilities, yet we tie ourselves down to socially-prescribed names and categories so we're acceptable to more people. We take on identities that no one has to think about, and that's probably how we become and why we remain men and women.

The first step in liberating ourselves from this meek-as-lambs culturally-imposed silence is for transgendered people to begin talking with each other, asking each other sincere questions, and listening intently.

Myths And Myth-Conceptions

A transgender subculture is at this writing developing, and it's subsequently giving rise to new folk tales and traditions of gender fluidity and ambiguity. For example:

» *We are the chosen people.*

This is the point of view of many groups, and is not the sole property of the transgendered. This point of view makes me nervous, and I usually disassociate myself from any group whose members proclaim some unique kinship to, or favored station with, some higher power.

» *We are normal men and women.*

Is there such a thing as a normal man or woman? I have this idea that there are only people who are fluidly-gendered, and that the norm is that most of these people continually struggle to maintain the illusion that they are one gender or another. So if someone goes through a gender change and then struggles to maintain a (new) rigid

gender, I guess that does make them normal. That's the
only way I can see the grounding to this myth.

>> *We are better men or women than men born men or women born women,
because we had to work at it.*

I don't know about this one—I think everyone has to
work at being a man or a woman. Transgendered people
are probably more aware of doing the work, that's all.
The concept of some nebulously "better" class of people
is not an idea of love and inclusion, but an idea of
oppression.

>> *We have an incurable disease.*

No, we don't.

>> *We are trapped in the wrong body.*

I understand that many people may explain their pre-
operative transgendered lives in this way, but I'll bet
that it's more likely an unfortunate metaphor that con-
veniently conforms to cultural expectations, rather than
an honest reflection of our transgendered feelings. As a
people, we're short on metaphors, any metaphors, and
when we find one that people understand, we stop looking. It's time for transgendered people to look for new
metaphors—new ways of communicating our lives to
people who are traditionally gendered.

>> *We are the most put-upon of people.*

I think this statement is sadly arrogant, and an admission of social ignorance. I heard this myth from a pre-
operative white, middle-class, male-to-female transsexual
who is a medical doctor. I guess she hadn't heard too

much about teenage African-American mothers on crack, or some other more "put-upon" people. Transsexuals get a lot of grief from nearly every level of this hierarchical culture, it's true, but it's important to maintain some perspective.

>> *That there* is *a transgender community.*

Someone asked me if the transgendered community is like the lesbian/gay communities. I said no, because the lesbian/gay communities are based on who one relates to, whereas the transgendered experience is different: it's about identity—relating to oneself. It's more an inward thing. When you have people together with **those** issues, the group dynamic is inherently very different.

—David Harrison, in conversation with
the author, 1993

We're at the beginning stages of a transgender community, but, at this writing, there are still only small groups of people who live out different aspects of gender. I'm extremely interested in seeing what develops, taking into account Harrison's analogy of personal and group dynamics. Just now, pockets of resistance to social oppression are forming, most often in conjunction with various gay and lesbian communities.

I *have* found an underground of male-to-female gender outlaws which already has its own unspoken hierarchy, definable from whatever shoes you happen to be standing in—high heels or Reeboks.

Post-operative transsexuals (those transsexuals who've had genital surgery and live fully in the role of another gender) look down on:
Pre-operative transsexuals (those who are living full or part time in another gender, but who've not yet had their genital surgery) who in turn look down on:

Transgenders (people living in another gender identity, but who have little or no intention of having genital surgery) who can't abide:

She-Males (a she-male friend of mine described herself as "tits, big hair, lots of make-up, and a dick.") who snub the:

Drag Queens (gay men who on occasion dress in varying parodies of women) who laugh about the:

Out Transvestites (usually heterosexual men who dress as they think women dress, and who are out in the open about doing that) who pity the:

Closet Cases (transvestites who hide their cross-dressing) who mock the post-op transsexuals.

The female-to-male groups, as well as some working-class transgender clubs that I've been associated with, seem to be more inclusive in their membership and attendance requirements than the mostly middle-class, mostly white examples cited above, and they're also less hierarchical in both club procedure and ways of relating to one another. Very few groups exist, however, that encompass the full rainbow that is gender outlawism, and sadly, groups still divide along the lines of male-to-female and female-to-male gender outlaws.

We are all longing to go home to some place we have never been—a place, half-remembered, and half-envisioned we can only catch glimpses of from time to time. Community. Somewhere, there are people to whom we can speak with passion without having the words catch in our throats. Somewhere a circle of hands will open to receive us, eyes will light up as we enter, voices will celebrate with us whenever we come into our own power. Community means strength that joins our strength to do the work that needs to be done. Arms to hold us when we falter. A

circle of healing. A circle of friends.
Someplace where we can be free.
　—Starhawk, *Dreaming the Dark: Magic,*
　　　　　Sex, and Politics, 1982

I'd like to be a member of a community some day. One of the reasons I didn't go through with my gender change for such a long time was the certain knowledge that I would be an outsider. All the categories of transgender find a common ground in that they each break one or more of the rules of gender: what we have in common is that we are gender outlaws, every one of us. To attempt to divide us into rigid categories ("You're a transvestite, and **you're** a drag queen, and **you're** a she-male, and on and on and on) is like trying to apply the laws of solids to the state of fluids: it's our fluidity that keeps us in touch with each other. It's our fluidity and the principles that attend that constant state of flux that could create an innovative and inclusive transgender community.

I really *would* like to be a member of a community, but until there's one that's based on the principle of constant change, the membership would involve more rules, and the rules that exist around the subject of gender are not rules I want to obey.

The Fly, the leader of a gang of criminals in the Wilma Theater production of the Brecht/Weill musical, **Happy End**, *1987, in Philadelphia, directed by Jiri Ziska. It was my first role in women's clothing, and I doubled as the male master of ceremonies.*

« 8 »

GENDER TERROR,
GENDER RAGE

*If transsexuality marks a response to the
dream of changing sex, it is also clearly the
object of dreaming, and even phantasizing,
in non-transsexuals. In the final analysis,
sexual difference, which owes much to sym-
bolic dualisms, belongs to the register of the
real. It constitutes an insuperable barrier,
an irreducible wall against which one can
bang one's head indefinitely.*

—Catherine Millot, *Horsexe: Essays on
Transexuality*, 1990

For a while, I thought that it would be fun to call what I do in life *gender
terrorism*. Seemed right at first—I and so many folks like me were ter-
rorizing the structure of gender itself. But I've come to see it a bit differently now— gender terrorists are not the drag queens, the butch dykes,
the men on roller skates dressed as nuns. Gender terrorists are not the
female to male transsexual who's learning to look people in the eye while
he walks down the street. Gender terrorists are not the leather daddies or
back-seat Betties. Gender terrorists are not the married men, shivering in
the dark as they slip on their wives' panties. Gender terrorists are those

who, like Ms. Millot, bang their heads against a gender system which is *real* and *natural*, and who then use gender to terrorize the rest of us. These are the real terrorists: the Gender Defenders.

[A]nything that undermines confidence in the scheme of classification on which people base their lives sickens them as though the very ground on which they stood precipitously dropped away. The vertigo produced by the loss of cognitive orientation is similar to that produced by the loss of physical orientation. Philosophic nausea, certain forms of schizophrenia, moral revulsion, negative experience, the horror of having violated a taboo, and the feeling of having been polluted are all manifestations of this mental **mal de mer**, *occasioned by the sudden shipwreck of cognitive orientation which casts one adrift in a world without structure.*

People will regard any phenomenon that produces this disorientation as "disgusting" or "dirty." To be so regarded, however, the phenomenon must threaten to destroy not only one of their fundamental cognitive categories but their whole cognitive system.

—Murray S. Davis, *Smut: Erotic Reality/Obscene Ideology*, 1983

That's what gender outlaws do: our mere presence is often enough to make people sick. Take that great scene in the film, *The Crying Game.* You know the scene: the one that got all the attention—the one you weren't supposed to talk about? The one with the (gasp) full penile nudity—on the body of what appeared to be a woman! To me, the telling aspect of the scene is not so much the revelation of the person as transgendered, as much as it was the nausea and vomiting by the guy who did the discovering. That's a fairly strong reaction in any language, any culture. Many transgendered people will tell you that's an all-too accurate reaction; one usually followed, as in *The Crying Game*, by a physical attack on the transgendered person. With all the talk centering on the movie at the time of its release, no one focused on the issue of revulsion. I think no one brought it up, because it would draw focus to the other side of revulsion: desire.

The revelation of Dil's gender ambiguity called into question both the sexual orientation (desire) and the gender identity of Fergus.

> Fergus' inner dialogue may have gone like this: "I'm really turned on by this woman, and that's how it should be—I'm male and I'm heterosexual." Then, as Dil disrobes, that inner voice might protest, "Wait! She's got a penis! She's a man!" And then the real awful truth may reveal itself like this: "Wait, I'm still attracted to this person, this man! But only women and faggots go for men—does that mean I'm a woman? Does it mean I'm homosexual?" Poor baby!

His vomiting can be seen not so much as a sign of revulsion as an admission of attraction, and the consequential upheaval of his gender identity and sexual orientation. The questioning of these heretofore unquestioned states of very personal identity would certainly result in nausea—the poor man's cognitive system had really been shaken up! I don't think *The Crying Game* is saying it's good to throw up when you find out someone is transgendered; I think the movie is brilliantly showing us that it's a common response.

And how about the public silence surrounding *The Crying Game*? When it was released in 1993, no one wanted to give away the "big secret." The last time there was such a furor about "don't give away the surprise ending," it was Hitchcock's *Psycho*, about another secretly transgendered person. The public response of "don't say a word" is more than "don't spoil the movie." What's to spoil, anyway? I knew about "the secret" before I went, and I thoroughly enjoyed the film. No, I think the "keep the secret" response on the part of the public was more a reflection of how the gender defenders of this culture would like to see transgendered people: as a secret, hidden away in some closet.

> The Gender Defender is someone who actively, or by knowing inaction, defends the status quo of the existing gender system, and thus perpetuates the violence of male privilege and all its social extensions. The gender defender, or gender terrorist, is someone for whom gender forms a cornerstone of their view of the world. Shake gender up for one of these folks, and you're in for trouble.

What Are They Afraid Of?

Because gender ambiguity and gender outlaws are made invisible in this culture, and because gender transgressors are by and large silent (and thus invisible), for reasons stated earlier, the defenders of gender rigidity lash out at the nearest familiar label: homosexuality and lesbianism, the points at which gender outsiders intersect with sexual outsiders.

Not surprisingly, there are no words for the terror and hatred of gender transgressors, and because no one has named it yet, it seems that there is no hatred. When they do name it, they'll probably call it "genderism" or something equally boring.

> So much violence is perpetrated in the name of that fear and that loathing. I've been trying to come up with a name for this phobia for a few years now, and the word has eluded me. **Transphobia** is one term in vogue with some transsexuals. Fear of crossing? Fear of transgressing? If this term were allowed that sort of breadth—that is including the fear and hatred of **any** kind of border-dwellers—then it might have some possibilities.

The acts of a gender defender are acts of violence against gender outsiders.

>> **Gay Bashing is one act of gender defenders.**

›› Have you seen a single gay man or lesbian walking down
the street recently?

›› How did you know or why did you suspect that they were
gay or lesbian?

›› Was it something they were doing sexually? Or something about their gender presentation?

›› Why do gay bashers pick out certain gays and lesbians
to bash?

›› **The attack on transsexuals by some cultural feminists is
another defense of gender.**

*All transsexuals rape women's bodies by
reducing the real female form to an artifact,
appropriating this body for themselves.
However, the transsexually constructed les-
bian-feminist violates women's sexuality and
spirit, as well. Rape, although it is usually
done by force, can also be accomplished by
deception. It is significant that in the case
of the transsexually constructed lesbian-
feminist, often he is able to gain entrance
and a dominant position in women's spaces
because the women involved do not know he
is a transsexual and he just does not happen to mention it.*

—Janice G. Raymond, *The Transexual
Empire*, 1979

Both Raymond and Millot generalize beyond what would be acceptable
practice in any academic work; that's a mark of their fanaticism. But
there's some historical, cross-cultural precedent for their concern that
transsexuals are bad for feminism: the Navajo *nadle*. The *nadle* is a sort of
transgendered male-to-female person, with a unique social function: the
nadle was often called upon to suppress the women's revolutions.

Neither Raymond nor Millot seem familiar with these wolves in chic clothing, but both implicitly fear the concept.

> The **nadle**'s role and value in mythology are male-oriented. Barren themselves, the **nadle** are useful as mediators, and, perhaps related to this, they serve as ferrymen. When there was a quarrel between the men and the women and the latter secluded themselves on one side of the river, the **nadle**, by deciding to bring the women back across, enabled the men to overcome the women. In doing this, they acted as [gender] strikebreakers or scabs, reversing the course of the age-old theme of the strike of one [gender] against the other.
>
> —Wendy O'Flaherty, Women, Androgynes, and other Mythical Beasts, 1980

I've seen some examples of what Raymond fears: male-to-female transsexuals entering "women-only" spaces, and attempting to assume a position of control and power. If Raymond herself has personally experienced that, I can empathize with her anger. My contention, however, is that it is not the transsexual person or even the issue of transsexuality that is bad for feminism: I think that what's bad for the future of feminism is male privilege, and I think that occasionally a male-to-female transsexual will carry more than a small degree of that over into their newly-gendered life. A better solution to this situation would be to point out what's going on, and to talk it through. I don't think male privilege has a place *anywhere*, and I think it would best be processed out of *any* environment.

Raymond and her supporters bring up the subject of deception. Personally, I agree that hiding, and not proclaiming one's transsexual status, is an unworthy stance, more heinous if one's invisible status is maintained with the purpose of gaining power. Transsexuals are mov-

ing, however, in the direction of openly embracing their borderline status—either willingly, or by the probing eye of public interest—and the
debate on being or not-being out as a transsexual is, at this writing,
heating up.

›› Segments of the Men's Movement defend gender.

> I'm talking about men who drum and chant in the woods
> to ward off the possibility of being called women. What's
> amusing is that lesbians had been drumming and chanting
> in the woods for well over a decade before Robert Bly and
> company got the bright idea to appropriate the practice
> and proclaim it "male."

›› The author of the "Helms Amendment" is definitely a gender defender!

*"None of the funds authorized to be appro-
priated for the National Endowment for the
Arts...may be used to promote, disseminate,
or produce materials which in the judgment
of the National Endowment for the
Arts...may be considered obscene, including
but not limited to, depictions of sadomasochism, homoeroticism, the sexual
exploitation of children, or individuals
engaged in sex acts and which, when taken
as a whole, do not have serious literary,
artistic, political or scientific value."*

—Senator Jesse Helms, Republican,
North Carolina

I'm not included in Senator Helms' amendment. I'm not included in
most legislation these days. But me and my people, we're the ones
they'd *want* to legislate against, if they could even begin to conceive of
us, because *we're* the ones who threaten their manhood. People have

underrated Gore Vidal's *Myra Breckinridge*, and the sequel *Myron*. In fact, the movie version of *Myra Breckenridge* has been called one of the worst movies of all time. I think it has a lot to do with the point Vidal makes: that the existence of transgendered people—people who exist sexually for pleasure, and not procreation—strikes terror at the heart of our puritanical Eurocentric culture. Vidal positions Myra as the voice and agent of doom for the traditional American male. I think he was on the mark, and I'd be proud to call Myra my sister.

I'm afraid that by spelling this all out the way I'm doing in this book, and the way other transgendered people are doing—I'm afraid we'll tip our hands. Could be fun, though, and it's much better than suffocating in the grip of the social disease called gender!

The Protection Racket

We can feel secure in the protection provided by a group, but that protection has its price. Compliance with the group often extends further than acceptance of the group's views to include participation in the attack on deviants by subtle (or not so subtle) disapproval, punishment, or rejection of any member who voices criticism of the consensus....[The] dissident is criticized as disloyal, lacking commitment, interfering with the important work of the group.
—Arthur J. Deikman, *The Wrong Way Home: Uncovering Patterns of Cult Behavior in American Society*, 1990

There's no current protection for the transgendered, no group dynamic strong enough to ward off possible attacks on individuals. I'm not looking forward to the police-

man's baton, the media's poison, or the assassin's bullet—sadly, these are almost inevitable in this world of
wave after wave of minorities rising up to confront the
dominant ideology.

This culture attacks people on the basis of being or not being correctly
gendered (having a politically correct body). It's when we get to a point
of knowing we're not gendered in the same way as our friends, relatives,
and co-workers—it's then that we get angry and start to do something
about gender.

›› What's your gender?

›› When did you decide that?

›› How much say do you have in your gender?

›› Is there anything about your gender or gender role that
   you don't like, or that gets in your way?

›› Are there one or two qualities about another gender that
   are appealing to you, enough so that you'd like to incorporate those qualities into your daily life?

›› What would happen to your life if you did that?

›› What would your gender be then?

›› How do you think people would respond to you?

›› How would you feel if they did that?

Gender Activism Begins With Gender Rage

"You're just jealous because **I'm** *a real*
freak, and **you** *have to wear a mask!"*
—The Penguin
"You just may be right." —Batman
   —Tim Burton, *Batman Returns*, 1993

Sometimes, it's not the fist in your belly that
   gets to you.
Sometimes, it's when they're quiet, even polite.
Sometimes, it's how they look at you day after day that

finally gets to you.
They squint at you, like they can't see.
It's as if by squinting
    they might get a better make on you.
If they're in a crowd, they shift their eyes
    so their friends can't tell they're looking at you.
    Real subtle.
You can read the fear behind the smirk,
The hatred just past the disgust.
You worry it's your paranoia.
and you always hope it's only your paranoia.
(Confidence, they've told you, helps you pass.)
But there's always one of them who looks at you
    with longing.
And that scares you the most,
Because if you let that longing into your heart, you have to
    accept yourself
        just the way you are.

It's not only people who intentionally transgress gender who get into trouble. Eventually the gender system lets everyone down. It seems to be rigged that way. Sometimes, even with all the time and effort we put into obeying the rules, we get hurt. We can get badly hurt by being a real man or a real woman.

So what happens to the person who finds out that he or she has been duped or disappointed by some aspect of gender? How does someone come to terms with some inner ambiguity of gender, and the demands of a rigid, nearly monolithic, universal gender system? This person could get closer to the gender outlaws who have previously been regarded as outsiders. This person would sense some common ground with the more obvious renegades of the gender system, usually some commonality in the area of gender role oppression. Bridging the gap between him or herself and the outlaws, the now former-gender-defenders can't devalue the outsider without devaluing him or herself. Instead of someone defending gender, we've now got someone who begins intentionally to bend gender.

›› What are you being denied on account of your gender?

›› What does a person of another gender have that you can't have?

And this brings up a great deal of anger. Because, we've suddenly positioned ourselves in the area previously marked "freaks only." We've chosen to stand with the oppressed. But standing with freaks never hurt anyone—it's when we agree that we *deserve* the oppression and the ridicule that accompanies the freak's position in the culture—that's when the wound is mortal.

> The first national television talk show I did was **Geraldo**. The subject was **Transsexual Regrets: Who's Sorry Now**. It was supposed to be about all these transsexuals who'd gotten fairly far along in their transformation, but were now changing their minds. I was there with psychologist Jayne Thomas to provide a little balance: we were the happy transsexuals. Somewhere around the time when an audience member asked me if I could "orgasm with that vagina," I realized that yep, I was a freak all right, but I was only a freak to the degree that I remained silent. When I spoke, I had a chance to educate, and, paradoxically, I became less of a freak.

We don't deserve the ridicule, the stares, the fist in our bellies. We are entitled to our anger in response to this oppression: our anger is a message to ourselves that we need to get active and change something in order to survive. So we resist the oppression, the violence—we resist the tendency of the culture to see us as a joke.

So now we're standing on the side of the freaks. Now what? If we can't call the freaks names anymore because we realize we're one of them, then we have to look back at our position as a former insider, and we begin to devalue *that*. We've now officially become activists. But outside or inside, it's still a side; and taking a side usually means taking the identity of a side, and there you have identity politics as one more rendering of a game called us-versus-them. In "transgender politics," as in any other identity politics, we look around for a "them." From the standpoint of the transgendered person, there's no shortage of "them," no shortage at all.

> A theatre critic in **The San Francisco Chronicle** once chided me for bringing a show about transsexualism to a lesbian and gay theater. "Preaching to the converted," he called it. Who or what did he think was in the audience? I tell you, I **wish** there had been an audience of transsexuals out there each night! I'd have felt a lot less lonely and vulnerable than I did. People make assumptions.

Loose Canons of Activism

One trouble in having only a few of "us," and a lot of "them," is that it's easy to hit out at the wrong "them." At this writing, some transgender activists are targeting lesbian separatists because these women have established something called "women-only spaces"; and a small number of these women will not brook the admission of transgendered women, whom the separatists don't see as women. In response to demands for inclusion by the transgendered, the women on the inside get angry and a war of epithets begins. It's a war about who's a man and who's a woman.

From what I can see, women inhabit "women only" spaces to heal from the oppression of their number by the larger culture, by men in particular, and because they don't see us as women, we're perceived as the other side of the binary: men. Perceived as men, we get in the way of their healing, and so we're excluded.

> The current phraseology is "women born women." We're told that only "women born women" are allowed into some space. Well, that's a problem. Aside from the obvious absurdity of a newborn infant being called a woman, the phrase "woman born woman" just throws us back

into the what's-a-woman question.

Some transsexuals take exclusion by lesbian separatists as oppression, but I don't think so. Lesbian oppression at the hands of the dominant ideology is not the same as the exclusion experienced by the transgendered at the hands of the lesbian separatists—lesbians just don't have the same economic and social resources with which to oppress the transgendered. I think both sides need to sit down and talk with one another, and I think both sides need to do some serious listening.

> I once stated this opinion in a San Francisco newspaper article. A small number of transgender activists called me a Nazi and a reactionary, and claimed I'd set "the cause" back years through that article. Their accusation was that I was giving fuel to "the enemy." I got harassing phone calls, and they threatened to demonstrate against my next theater piece. Like I said, I don't speak for all transgendered people.

A free society is one where it is safe to be unpopular.

—Adlai Stevenson

I think that anger and activism mix about as well as drinking and driving. When I'm angry, I don't have the judgment to select a correct target to hit out against. I do believe that anger is healthy, that it can lead to a recognition of the *need* for action, but activism itself is best accomplished by level heads who can help steer others' anger toward correct targets. A correct target is the group that has both the will and the power to oppress you wherever you go. The correct target for any successful transsexual rebellion would be the gender system itself. But transsexuals won't attack that system until they themselves are free of the need to participate in it.

> Movements tend to coalesce around a particular moment of rebellion. The transgender moment of rebellion has not

yet come, and transgendered people are growing more and more restless. But the transgender Stonewall or Selma, Alabama is not going to come about by attacking the gay and lesbian community, or even lesbian separatists, outlaws like ourselves. In Selma, and at the Stonewall, members of the minority group stood up to the real forces of oppression: the police state.

It does hurt, being excluded or even attacked by other oppressed groups, and it makes me feel a shame I thought I'd gotten over a long time ago. It's not what people say when they exclude me and my people, or how they say it, but rather it's a very long ache that I don't believe will stop until there's a whole lot more room in the world for difference. Sometimes it's a seemingly insignificant act of exclusion that will tip the scale and turn someone from insider to outsider, like the one that really got to me.

When I first went through my gender change, I was working for an IBM subsidiary in Philadelphia. The biggest quandary there was "which bathroom is it going to use?" To their credit, most of the people in my office didn't really care; it was the building manager who was tearing his hair out over this one. I suppose he felt I would terrorize the women in their bathroom, and lie in waiting for the men in **their** bathroom. Finally, a solution was reached: even though I worked on the 11th floor of a large office building, I would use a bathroom on the seventh floor. The seventh floor had been under construction, but for lack of funds they simply stopped construction; no one worked on that floor. Piles of plaster and wiring littered the floor, and pools of water lay everywhere. But there was a working bathroom in the very back of that floor, and that's where they sent me. No one ever cleaned it, no one kept it stocked. It was poorly lit and it was scary. Isn't it amazing the lengths we'll go to in order to maintain the illusion that there are only two genders, and that these genders

> must remain separate? Most gender outlaws have some
> similar bathroom horror story. It's all part of what
> Marjorie Garber calls "urinary segregation."

Something happens, some final bit that lights up the injustice of the
gender system, and in that flash, we see that the emperor is wearing no
clothes. That this either/or gender system we've got is truly oppressing
us. That happens, and we snap; we begin to fight.

>> ›› Have you ever been teased or baited by reason of acting
>> outside your assigned gender role?
>> ›› Where do you think the sanctions for that teasing or
>> baiting come from?

There are a lot of ways to fight, and transgendered people these days
are coming together in the common fight for the right to express our
genders freely. Where once we met only in drag bars or social teas,
we're now meeting at protest marches and in consciousness-raising
groups.

>> ›› Would you like to meet other people who feel the same
>> way you do about gender?
>> ›› Would you like to hear you're not the only one?
>> ›› Would you like to know you've got a history in this
>> world?
>> ›› Do you think that might make you smile?

We meet to discuss ways and means of securing our freedom. In this
struggle for our freedom of expression there comes a point where the
gender system reveals itself to be not only oppressive, but silly. When
we see how ridiculous it is, we can truly begin to dismantle it.

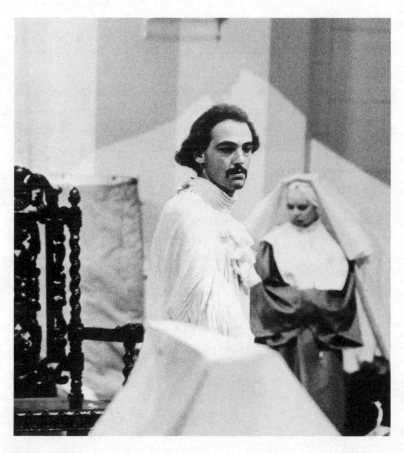

*The Marquis de Sade in the 1969 Brown University production of **Marat/Sade**, directed by John Emigh.*

« 9 »

SEND IN THE CLOWNS

A few weeks after I told my mother that I was going to become her daughter, she called me with a question. "Are you sure," she asked, "this change of yours isn't just another role? You've always been an actor, is this just another part, maybe your most challenging one?" At the time, I was offended. How dare she, I asked myself, compare my life's struggle with some part! But, looking back, it really was a good question. Thanks, mom.

Real gender freedom begins with fun. Here, you get what might be called The Gender Blender, a sort of whirling confusion of leather and rhinestones. These creatures do not spring full-born from the forehead of the culture; gender blenders earn their feather boa wings step by step, feather by feather.

The easiest way to spot a newly transgendered person is that he or she moves just a bit slower than most people; he or she is unlearning old ways of moving, and picking up new ways of moving. So one of the first things you try to do is to move at a normal pace, because you don't want to be laughed at. You don't want the high school kids pointing and yelling. You don't want to see the looks of disgust on people's faces. So you learn how to blend in. It's called "passing."

> [The standup comic] seems to know no fear
> of humiliation and thus appears to be danger-
> ously outside the boundaries of social control.
> —David Marc, Comic Visions: Television
> Comedy and American Culture, 1989

Humiliation is a whip of the defenders of gender. Humiliation is sanctioned at virtually every level of the culture: people can laugh at a transgendered person; but when there's no fear of being humiliated for one's portrayal of gender, there's less opportunity for the culture to exert control.

> I was on my way to a surgeon's office on the upper East Side. It was rush hour, and the train station was packed. There was a large crowd of people avoiding an old man who was standing in the middle of the passageway. I heard his voice up ahead, above the noise of the crowd.
>
> "Sir, twenty-five cents, please."
>
> Or he'd say, "Lady, got a quarter?"
>
> I was reaching into my bag for some change, just as the motion of the crowd brought me almost face to face with him.
>
> He was so grimy.
>
> He stank of urine and wine.
>
> He looked right at me.
>
> "Lady?" he said.
>
> "Mister?" he said.
>
> "Say, what the fuck are you?" he said. And he began to laugh.
>
> He laughed. And he laughed. He just laughed. And the crowd carried me further down the passageway, and I could still hear him laughing.

We're taught to pay attention to the humiliation, because it can be enforced by violence, the other whip of the system. Violence against transgendered people makes freedom from the fear of humiliation tricky to say the least. So you have some choices: you can get real good at hiding, or you can get beat up. You can commit suicide—or you learn how to laugh. There are actually quite a few opportunities to laugh, but fear keeps us from looking at those opportunities.

Cross-culturally, the individuals who have freed themselves from the fear of humiliation are clowns, fools, jesters, and tricksters. This can be Coyote, Uncle Tolpa, Br'er Rabbit, Raccoon Dog, or any number of documented practitioners of what Scoop Nisker calls *crazy wisdom* in cultures around the world.

The great fool, like Einstein, wonders about the obvious and stands in awe of the ordinary, which makes him capable of revolutionary discoveries about space and time. The great fool lives outside the blinding circle of routine, remaining open to the surprise of each moment. We are the foolish ones, complacent in our understanding. We take for granted the miraculous dance of creation, but the great fool continuously sees it for the first time. The revelations of the great fool often show us where we are going, or—more often—where we are.
—Scoop Nisker, *Crazy Wisdom*, 1990

What do fools have in common? Well, they don't play by the rules, they laugh at most rules, and they encourage us to laugh at ourselves. Their pranks of substituting one thing for another create instability and uncertainty, making visible the lies imbedded in a culture. Fools demonstrate the wisdom of simplicity and innocence. These are valuable crafts, these are skills we could use in our problem-laden world.

The market value of comedy ascends in the face of a plausible end to history.
—David Marc, *Comic Visions: Television Comedy and American Culture*, 1989

Any healthy civilization would certainly have people performing these fool skills at every level of the culture. In *our* civilization, the only people doing these things are considered trouble-makers, whatever their line of work.

The only true art is art that raises questions
and implicates people.
                              —Holly Hughes,
                    Sphinxes Without Secrets, 1990

There's room in our Eurocentric culture for a class of clowns, jesters, tricksters, and fools. In fact, there are a lot of positions open. Since very few people are volunteering, since people laugh at us anyway, and since we have such wit, charm, and impeccable fashion sense, I think transgendered people should move right into these roles.

> I mentioned this once in writing, and it raised the question of how does someone who's not an actor or writer, and who (sensibly) doesn't want to **be** an actor or a writer, get along in this role. I think it's just a matter of incorporating a sense of humor into our daily lives. I think it has a lot to do with taking the tendency people have for laughing at us, and laughing **first**, so as to highlight and defuse that mechanism. That doesn't take talent; it takes living life at one's right size. It takes an admission of one's outsider status, and a wish to help others expand their points of view. It takes compassion.

Who Are the Fools?

The fool's role can be taken on at the secretary's desk as easily as on the stage. The clown can perform in a circus or on a bus. The jester can take the ear of a king, or the ear of a neighbor. The trickster can fool the Congress of the United States, or the folks down at the general store.

Today's more widely-known fools are the solo performers, monologists, standups, anyone who addresses or performs before any audience,

like the odd instructor or professor. These folks are the twentieth century's answer to the roving minstrel or countryside jester. Some of the
many gender blenders of our times are fools like these:

>> **Sandy Stone**, singled out for attack by Janice Raymond in her
book, *The Transsexual Empire*, in 1979. After a dozen years of
recovery and research, Stone is once more back on the scene with
her rib-tickling, devilish essay, "The Empire Strikes Back: A
Posttranssexual Manifesto."

>> **Elvis Herselvis**, a San Francisco-based lesbian writer and Elvis
impersonator; and **Glamoretta Rampage**, (AKA San Francisco-
based writer and performer, Justin Bond), the charming wife of
Elvis Herselvis.

>> **Shelley Mars**, performance artist and Drag King *extraordinaire*
from New York City.

>> Writer, director **Ingrid Wilhite**, whose two films *Fun With a
Sausage*, and *The Mister Sisters*, stretch the limits of lesbian identity, and nicely blur the lines of gender identity and sexual orientation.

>> **The Sisters of Perpetual Indulgence, Inc.**, is, per their own lit-
erature "…a controversial order of gay, bisexual, and transgender
'nuns' of various religious backgrounds founded in Iowa in the
mid-1970s." The Sisters hold various fund-raising events to benefit various AIDS-related groups.

SISTER SAM WANTS YOU!
JOIN QUEER ARMY TODAY!
NO WARS—FABULOUS PARADES!
　　　　—from a recruitment flier by
The Sisters of Perpetual Indulgence, 1992

>> The late **Doris Fish**, Australia and San Francisco; the late
"Tippi," San Francisco; the late **Ethyl Eichelberger**, New York:
three transgendered performance artists with AIDS who died
within a year of each other.

There are perhaps better-known kings and queens of drag. Milton

Berle, Nipsey Russell, and Lucille Ball come to mind immediately. But I think that using drag on stage as a gimmick, a *shtick*, is an appropriation; it's different than living a transgendered life and then using that life for material on stage or screen. The contrast between transgender as gimmick and transgender as life marks one major difference between mainstream theater and what might be called queer theater.

There's a strength in knowing we have our own comics, our own jokers. But here it gets tricky. The pressure and temptation is to create art or politics for a particular group, which is in turn based on some inflexible identity: special interest groups, identity politics, whatever you want to call it. The group becomes loyal audience, supporters, and followers, if for no other reason than the fool is speaking their language, performing their lives.

But this is so important: the fool became a fool by flexing the rules, the boundaries of the group, and this is antithetical to the survival dynamic of most groups. A group remains a group by being inflexible: once it stretches its borders, it's no longer the same group. A fool, in order to survive, must not identify long with any rigidly-structured group. When more and more of the fool's work is done for a particular identity-based group, then the fool becomes *identified* with the group. The fool is indeed foolish who serves a special interest, and will quickly cease being a fool.

So where do all these transgender fools go, if not to lead or participate in some grand and glorious transgender revolution? They climb yet another step on the ladder of transgender evolution: they move toward some spiritual awareness and practice.

*We must never forget that art is not a form
of propaganda, it is a form of truth.*
            —John Fitzgerald Kennedy

« 10 »

FIRST YOU DIE, AND THEN
YOU GET THEIR ATTENTION

There are fools, there are fools, and there are fools. Where the traditional fool blurs the lines between genders, the shaman sees no lines. To the shaman, or holy fool, there's no us vs. them: in the shaman's eyes, we're somehow united. The shaman could be called a gender transcender.

Gender enlightenment begins with death. The shaman, cross-culturally, is someone who dies (literally or figuratively), has a brush with the spirit world, and returns to this world. There can be all sorts of death for the shaman.

The night before my genital surgery, I cut myself. I wear a small labrys around my neck. It's a double-headed ax, a symbol of goddess culture reputedly popular with Amazon warriors. I cut myself lightly across my left wrist with one blade and above my heart with the other blade. I was killing that part of me I considered to be a man. This was the final blow; it was my personal ritual. The next morning, I was given a shot of antihistamine to calm me down and to stop me from dripping from places that might be inconvenient to the surgeon. I was placed on the surgical cart and wheeled into the operating room. Lying on my back, I could only see the lights in the ceiling going by one by one. I remembered lying on some roughly-hewn cart, staring upward at the sun and the sky. Inside the operating room, the nurse anesthesiologist gave me another shot and told me to count backwards from one hundred. I got to ninety-six and then I died.

I woke up once during the procedure: I felt a sharp pain in what had once been my left testicle. Some more anesthesia, and I was dead again.

When I was very young, I would pray each night to wake up and be a girl. I'd add that part at the end of "Now I lay me down to sleep...." I remember waking from death back in my hospital bed and realizing that my old childhood prayer had come true. I reached for my Tarot deck and selected a card at random—Ace of Cups: Happiness.

What's supposed to happen in the instant/eternity between death and re-birth is that the spirits give the shaman a portion of the truth to take back to this world—a tiny grain of sand from the vast beaches of universal truth. But there's a catch. The shaman can only hang on to that portion of the truth if she or he tells it to others. If the shaman fails to reveal that portion of the truth continually to others, then the shaman is driven mad by the spirits.

This all sounded fairly esoteric until I put it into the terms of my very un-esoteric life. I died a virtual death, not only on the operating table, but in terms of a key aspect of my identity, and then I was reborn into the world. For me, the in-between place itself was the truth I was made aware of: the existence of a place that lies outside the borders of what's culturally acceptable.

But here's the kicker: I was born into a world that tells people like me to be silent, to not reveal that I'm transsexual, to not reveal my truth. It's the therapeutic lie that eventually causes us to go mad: it's hiding, passing, and being silent that makes us crazy. Silence does equal death—that principle applies to any situation involving a culturally-mandated silence, and it's important to observe the phenomenon of the shaman in *any* virtual death/rebirth situation.

The shamanic model can be seen in the sobering-up of an alco-holic—which would account for the importance that recovering alco-holics place on telling their stories. The shamanic phenomenon can be heard in the coming-out story of a lesbian woman or gay man. Have you noticed that shortly after making friends with a lesbian or gay man, they tell you their coming-out story? His or her portion of the world's truth is somewhere in that story.

Sometimes, the Message *Is* the Message

What if some re-born shaman enters the world, begins to relate that portion of the truth, and people don't or can't understand?

> There's no guarantee that anyone is going to **believe** the shaman, even if the shaman speaks up: look at Cassandra, cursed by Apollo to tell the truth and when she did, no one would believe her. Cassandra says "I tell the truth, and they won't listen!" She probably had an attitude problem.

I think it's up to the shaman to figure out the way to make that truth understandable in this world. I think it's *how you tell the truth*, as much as what you're saying: that's Marshall McCluhan's medium as message as massage, form being every bit as important as content. Culture itself is an acceptable performance of a truth, or truth with an easy learning curve—people understand the culture. The shaman needs to communicate/perform that truth in such a way that the culture can hear it.

Science is a way of talking about the universe in words that bind it to a common reality. Magic is a method of talking to the universe in words that it cannot ignore. The two are rarely compatible.

—Neil Gaiman,
The Invisible Labyrinth, 1993

The truth of the shaman is the performance of the shaman, a performance that can't be ignored. With this performance, the shaman performs (creates) the culture. The essential tool of the shaman is paradox: a presence which is absent or, equally, an absence which is present.

The phenomenon of transexualism is both a confirmation of the constructedness of gender and a secondary recourse to essentialism—or, to put it a slightly different way, transexualism demonstrates that essentialism is a cultural construction.
Marjorie Garber, Vested Interests: Cross Dressing and Cultural Anxiety, 1992

Finally, You Kiss It Better

The value of the paradox is its ability to tie together two seemingly opposing forces or ideas—to bind two edges of a torn and bleeding wound. This kind of healing is traditional in any shamanic culture. Like good art and good sex, good healing can be transformational, blurring the lines between life and death. The healing acts of a gender transcender, or shaman, might begin with the dissolving of gender and gender boundaries. But gender, while it's a basic building block to our culture, is very likely not the final challenge for anyone who truly wants to fix the mess we've gotten ourselves into.

›› *Basic health and well-being mean the panoramic perception of all levels of being.*
›› *Healing means healing culture first, then people, and finally sickness.*
›› *Holiness means feeling many—all— spheres of existence within oneself.*
—Holger Kalweit, Shamans, Healers, and Medicine Men, 1992

The Catch, and How to Avoid It

There's a trap for shamans: there's a cultural tendency to deify the shaman as role model, pop icon, guru, or literally goddess or god. Take, for example, the deification of the ambiguously-gendered Marlene Dietrich or Michael Jackson. Deification fixes the shaman into a particular role or identity, with no room to move around, no room to grow. Like the fool, the shaman can't be bound up in any single identity; the shaman can't take sides or be part of any identity politics. The shaman needs to seek broader and broader groups of people to serve—by staying in a fixed time and place, the shaman's message will only be repeated over and over again to those who've already heard it, and then the madness sets in. The shaman needs to remain outside the binary, in some third space, a space that constantly shifts and changes.

The "third" is that which questions binary thinking and introduces crisis...[T]he "third" is a mode of articulation, a way of describing a space of possibility. Three puts in question the idea of one: of identity, self-sufficiency, self-knowledge.
  —Marjorie Garber, Vested Interests: Cross Dressing and Cultural Anxiety, 1992

The concept of the "third" is the concept of the outlaw, who subscribes to a dynamic of change, outside any given dichotomy.

I think anyone who regularly walks along a forbidden boundary or border (gay/straight, sober/drunk, female/male, black/white, etc.) has the potential to attain some degree of spiritual awareness. The task for those who take that road is, usually, to point a way out of struggle and suffering for as many people as possible, and that can best be accomplished by raising questions and implicating people.

We raise different questions depending on where we live. For example, I live at the fun-filled intersection of art, politics, class, and the academy. But because I'm not really a member of any of these groups, I raise questions like:

Economics—

›› If wealth and power are important, and if in this world wealth and power belong to men, then why did I cease being a man and give up that wealth and power?

›› What is the value of wealth and power?

Sexuality—

›› If men are supposed to love women and women are supposed to love men, then what am I if I love women?

›› And what are you if you are attracted to me?

›› What are we if we become lovers, you and I?

›› What is the nature of your desire?

Rather than wallow in self-pity or boil in some cauldron of rage and injustice, I think it's time for transgendered people to come together under our own banner: a banner that would include anyone who cares to admit their own gender ambiguities, a banner that includes all sexualities, races and ethnicities, religions, ages, classes, and states of body, a banner of the Third.

I think it's time for us to use our status as Third to bring some harmony into the world. Like other border outlaws, transgendered people are here to open some doorway that's been closed off for a long long time. We're gatekeepers, nothing more.

The Tao gives birth to One.
One gives birth to Two.
Two gives birth to Three.
Three gives birth to all things.

      —Lao-Tzu, *Tao-Te Ching*

Before going through with my surgery, before creating myself in Third, I asked questions, as many as possible, as many as I could think of. And I wrote down all the questions that people asked me. Before creating a Third space, it might be a good idea to make sure that all the questions that need asking actually get asked, as many as possible.

a gender interrogatory

Beyond questions like "Can you orgasm with that vagina?" there are questions that can actually make it easier to live a life in harmony with this world, out of the closet, and into the sunshine. These are some of the questions I could think up. I welcome any other questions like these: you can write me care of my publisher, or e-mail me directly at OutlawGal@AOL.com.

Warrant Officer Al Bornstein, First Mate aboard the sea-going yacht Apollo, flagship of the Church of Scientology.

« 11 »

THE FIRST QUESTION
or, They Have Those Funny, Staring Eyes

The first question needs a lot of space all to itself. The first question is the one that seems to get asked the least frequently: namely, why in the world are we hanging on to gender, and to our gender systems?

> I heard once that "Why?" is not a spiritual question. Perhaps not. But it **is** a political question, and politics seems to be as good a step as any on the road to spirituality.

Given any binary, it's fun to look for some hidden third, and the reason why the third was hidden says a lot about a culture. The choice between two of something is not a choice at all, but rather the opportunity to subscribe to the value system which holds the two presented choices as mutually exclusive alternatives. Once we choose one or the other, we've bought into the system that perpetuates the binary. When for example, I lived my life saying I was a man or a woman, I was tacitly supporting all the rules of the gender system that defines those two identities. I supported those rules in order to belong, or rather to *not* be an outsider, a non-belonger.

> Imagine belonging to gender in the same way that we belong to:
> The Kiwanis

Book-of-the-Month Club
The Democratic Party
A health club
A jury
A credit union
A frequent flier program
The military
A corporation
A singles club
A 12-step program
The gender system we practice in the Eurocentric cul-
ture of the twentieth century is the **real** Boys Club and
Girls Club!

I began to analyze gender dynamics in terms of group dynamics. One
fascinating point stood out as relevant to both gender and group
dynamics, providing a link between the two: compliance within a group
is set by the naming of good and bad behavior; the former is laudable,
the latter is punishable. *Either/or* is used as a control mechanism, as in,
"Either you live up to our high standards here in the club, or you're
membership will be revoked."

*"Ladies" are the kind of people who won't let
my girlfriend use the public ladies' room, thinking she's not a woman. Oh, but they're not
going to let her use the men's room either—
they're not going to let her be a man either. If
she's not a man, and she's not a woman, then
what is she? Once I asked my mother what fire
was: a solid, liquid or gas? And she said it
wasn't any one of those things—it was something that happened to things: a force of
nature, she called it.*

*Maybe that's what she is: a force of nature.
For sure she is something that happened to me.*
—Holly Hughes, *Clit Notes*, 1993

It's Just Like...Family, yeah...Family, that's it!

What if the bi-polar gender system *really was a group*, just like the Elks, or the weekly bridge club? And if its members were blindly following rules that they neither question nor were even capable of challenging, then the group becomes more like a cult—instead of the Knights of Columbus, we've got something more like the Branch Davidians. There are patterns, both structural and behavioral, common to cults. For a long time, I was a member of Scientology, so perhaps I'm sensitive to recognizing those patterns, even in groups not traditionally defined as cults.

The more I thought about it, the more I loved the idea of looking at gender as a cult, so I put it to a few tests. For example: cults, like most groups, need to defend their boundaries, their borders, and gender, as a cult, would need to do the same.

> It was really difficult to leave the group of...what should we call it? The gendered? Sure. It was really difficult to leave that group when I left off being male. I cannot think of many gendered people who encouraged me or even wished me well. In the same way that some cults keep their followers under lock and key, the gendered keep their number under tight control and surveillance. To lose a member (did I say that?) would be unthinkable.

Compliance with a group often means demonstrating one's allegiance through round-the-clock participation in the forwarding of the group's goals. Some minority communities demand this in the name of activism. In a cult, this day-and-night participation is often a requirement for continued membership. Similarly, within the cult of gender, members are required to weave the continual maintenance of the cult into their daily lives. Questions can go a long way toward breaking cult patterns.

> ›› Do you ever go to sleep at night wondering what gender you are?
>
> ›› Have you ever seriously questioned which bathroom to

›› use—men's or women's?

›› Do you buy your clothes mostly from some gender-specific store or department of a store?

›› Do you belong to or support some men-only or women-only club?

›› Do you think I'm a former man, and that I'm now a woman?

›› Do you think I'm still a man?

›› Have you examined your own gender and decided beyond a shadow of a doubt, based on examination, that you really are that one gender?

›› Do you think you're that gender naturally?

In some cults, demonstrating allegiance frequently means attacking the enemies of the cult.

[The] dissident [in any group] is criticized as disloyal, lacking commitment, interfering with the important work of the group.
    —Arthur J. Deikman, *The wrong Way Home: Uncovering Patterns of Cult Behavior in American Society*, 1990

And so we have a good excuse for violence in the name of gender. The reason for exclusion by the dominant culture of both homosexuality and gender ambiguity has less to do, I think, with sexual orientation than it does with gender role. When a gay man is bashed on the street, it's unlikely that the bashers are thinking of the gay man butt-fucking anyone or in fact being butt-fucked. It has little to do with imagining that man sucking cock. It has a lot to do with seeing that man violate the rules of gender in this culture. The first commandment in this culture for men is "Thou shalt not be a woman." And the corresponding commandment for a woman in this culture is "Thou shalt not be a man."

›› Do you think you have it in you to be a man?

›› Do you think you have it in you to be a woman?

›› Have you ever thought what it might be like to be neither for a day? An hour? One minute?

The most obviously violent structure within the cult of gender is sexism, misogyny. Misogyny is necessary to maintain the cult of gender,
the struggle to be one or the other. The dynamic is similar to the power
structure of this country needing an enemy, be it Hitler, an evil empire,
or a Hitler-like madman.

Growing up, the one thing that was consistent in my family, and in the families of all my friends, was an interesting form of misogyny. It was the one area in which I was
consistently told **NO**. No, you cannot behave like, look
like, or be a girl.

Gender as a System of Oppression

A particularly insidious aspect about gender—our gender system here
in the West, and perhaps for the planet as a whole—is that it is an
oppressive class system made all the more dangerous by the belief that
it is an entirely natural state of affairs. In this sense, gender is no different a form of class oppression than the caste system in India or
apartheid in South Africa. Those systems have long been held to be
"natural," and the way of the world in their respective cultures, based as
they are on the concept of the possibility of a pure identity.

Purity of identity is essential to modern-day identity politics, where-
in membership is only permitted after proof of a pure identity. That
holds true whether we're talking left wing or right wing politics. What,
after all, are the differences between demanding racial purity, ethnic
purity, ideological, moral or religious purity, and in the case of gender,
gender purity. What is purity anyway? Who gets to decide? Members of
the club assume *they're* pure, and it's only us outsiders who wonder what
we have to do in order to be allowed in.

In going from male to female, I discovered that men don't
seem to think about gender in the same way women do.

The preferred gender in our patriarchal society is male, and so males mostly take gender for granted, most men do not try to analyze what it means to be male. Even the men's movement seems more predicated on a desire to not be drawn into some web of femininity, rather than a desire to **question** the construct of male identity. Women, on the other hand, have been taught that they're the "second sex," the distaff gender, so their lives are an almost daily struggle with the concept of gender. The trap for women is the system itself: it's not men who are the foe so much as it is the bi-polar gender system that keeps men in place as more privileged.

Struggle and privilege, insiders and outsiders—these are some fairly common phenomena—but common to what? Cults? Well, yes, but as cute as the analogy may be, and as wickedly accurate some of the points may be, gender as cult is not a one-to-one correspondence. Then it hit me that gender struggles have historically failed to reach their goals, whereas class conflicts have historically had some degree of success.

The progress of women's rights in our culture, unlike other types of "progress," has
always been strangely reversible.
   —Ann Douglas, The Feminization of
         American Culture, 1977

It's time to call the persistent clash of genders what it really is: a class conflict within a dangerously invisible and pervasive cult-like class system. Gender is indeed a group, a club, a church—but it operates as a class system, pervasively, throughout the culture.

The continued oppression of women proves only that in any binary there's going to be one up and one down. The struggle for equal rights must include the struggle to dismantle the binary.

I got real curious about my position as former-man and not-quite-woman. Where did that place me in the gender/class struggle that was daily spinning itself out in our culture?

Paul Fussell, in his book *Class* outlines nine different classes in the U.S. He then devotes his final chapter to something he calls an "X" class: people who manage to live outside the class system. Try substituting the word "gender" for the word "class" in the following paragraph.

"X" people are better conceived as belonging to a category than a class because you are not born an X person, as you are born and reared a prole or a middle. You become an X person, or, to put it more bluntly, you earn X-personhood by a strenuous effort of discovery in which curiosity and originality are indispensable. And in discovering that you can become an X person you find the only escape from class. Entering category X often requires flight from parents and forebears....X people can be described as "self-cultivated."

–Paul Fussell, *Class*, 1984

Gender, Class, and Power

In the either/or gender class system that we call male and female, the structure of one-up, one-down fulfills the requisite for a power imbalance. It became clear that the reason that the bipolar gender system continues to exist, and is actively and tenaciously held in place, is that the bi-polar gender system is primarily a venue for the playing out of a power game. It's an arena in which roughly half the people in the world can have power over the other half.

Without the structure of the bi-polar gender system, the power dynamic between men and women shatters. People would not have gender to use as a hierarchical framework, and nearly half the members of the bipolar gender system would probably be at quite a loss. They believe (foolishly I think) that the power they have and exert over others is a good thing and they want to hang on to it, they're terrified of losing this stuff. What I'm talking about is what's been called "male privilege." And I think this is the crux of the gender issue; this is what's holding gender in place: people who have and exert male privilege just don't want to give it up. I think that male privilege is the glue that holds the system together.

> People ask me what it was like to have had that kind of privilege, what it was like to lose it, why in the world did I give it up. To have it was like taking drugs, to get rid of it was like kicking a habit. I gave it up because it was destroying me and the people I loved.

"Male privilege" is assuming one has the right to occupy any space or person by whatever means, with or without permission. It's a sense of entitlement that's unique to those who have been raised male in most cultures—it's notably absent in most girls and women. Male privilege is not something that's given to men in this culture; it's something that men take. It's not that women don't have the ability to have and wield this privilege; some do. It's that in most cases, this privilege is withheld from them culturally and emotionally. Male privilege is woven into all levels of the culture, from unearned higher wages to more opportunities in the workplace, from higher quality, less expensive clothing to better bathroom facilities. Male privilege extends into sexual harassment, rape, and war. Combine male privilege with capitalism (which rewards greed and acquisition) and the mass media (which, owned by capitalists, highlights only the rewards of acquisition and makes invisible its penalties), and you have a juggernaut that needs stopping by any means. Male privilege is not the exclusive province of men; there are some few women who have a degree of this horrifying personality trait. Male privilege is, in a word, violence.

> An interesting way to negotiate a truce in the "war between the sexes" in the U.S. would be to mandate not an increase in wages for women, but rather a **decrease**

in wages for **men** to the level of any woman holding a
similar position. Use the money thus saved to repay the
U.S. deficit. I wonder how far that would fly in a male-
dominated Senate and House of Representatives?

Whatever the idea might be which hopes to end the suffering of women
on this planet, it's going to require men giving up privilege, and then all
of us giving up this rigid bi-polar gender system. Un-privileging is a
necessary prior condition for the deconstruction of the gender system.

More on Male Privilege

I'm involved in a delightful, protracted correspondence with Caitlin
Sullivan, radical butch dyke and freelance editor. She asks me challenging questions, which turn me on as much as any flirtation.

*Re the male privilege thing. Why are the
male-to-females so reluctant to admit this?
Do they want to pretend they were never
male? By the same token, could you
elaborate on what it felt like to lose that
privilege? You've described having it—were
you aware at the time? What were the ways
you noticed you didn't have it anymore? And,
what have you retained as a result of having had it? Confidence springs to mind, is
that true?*
    —Caitlin Sullivan, in correspondence
                with the author, 1993

I'm not sure I'm any more or less confident as a result of having lived a
life with male privilege, Caitlin. Maybe it's more that I know how to act
confident even when I'm not.

I don't know why some male-to-females you met were reluctant to
admit having had (or having) male privilege. For me, I just wasn't *aware* of
any general impunity when I had it. I can understand men looking baf-

fled when women accuse them of exercising male privilege; it's like many white people who look blank when confronted with their racism. It's also like traditionally-gendered people who look blank when confronted with their fear and mistreatment of people who are differently gendered.

I didn't "lose" my male privilege so much as I made a conscious decision to get rid of it, and I didn't get rid of it all at once; it's an attitude that is insidiously pervasive. Right now the point where my vestigial privilege surfaces is when I'm driving: I can be quite a terror. Sigh.

It took my becoming a woman to discover my "male behavior"—that is, exhibiting male privilege. When I was first coming out, I used to hang out mostly with women. Any act of mine that was learned male behavior stuck out like a sore thumb. Things like leaping up and taking charge, even when it wasn't called for; things like using a conversation like a sledge hammer; things like assuming that everyone owed me special consideration for my journey through a gender change—I still shudder at my arrogance. Some might say none of that's male. Well, I learned it when I was a guy, and I was the only one exhibiting that behavior when I was in the company of women, so if it's not *exclusively* male, it's real close. My friend Michelle Moran laughs and says she can spot the male sense of entitlement in male-to-female transsexuals who *insist* on acceptance as women. "They wanna be women," she jokes, "Let 'em start with a good dose of humility."

I noticed I didn't have much remaining male privilege by the slow dawning of peacefulness in my life. That may sound flaky, but the fact is I'm nowhere near as territorial and possessive as I used to be. I'm not as frantic to get or hold on to something as I once was. I still want things. I still go after things. But I use force infrequently now. For me, that's a perk of having gotten rid of male privilege. The shortcomings are obvious: lower pay, less security, more fear on the streets, less opportunity in the job market. All those drawbacks made me look at the value of what I'd lost. Do I really want to take part in a culture that places a higher value on greed and acquisition than on peace and shared growth?

> One of the things that makes me, and others like me, dangerous is that we do speak up. We break the silence imposed on our people. And what we talk about is the

very real oppression of women. In my case, I'm not theorizing about it like a man would...I've come from a place of privilege and I am now experiencing life as very different and non-privileged. And there are plenty of people who wouldn't want me to talk about this. I break this silence and the silence is what keeps the binary, and the oppression done in its name, in place.

This book, and the many other words, acts, art, and politics of other gender activists attest that it's a time of cultural readiness for these theories—these ambiguities. We might actually be making more progress in the area of gender than we're aware of: more and more people are asking questions, and that's a good sign. We just haven't been measuring that progress by a yardstick that everyone can agree on. We haven't dared to name a goal: probably something like "a society free from the constraints of non-consensual gender."

To discover what headway we are in fact making, we not only need to name a goal, we need to develop a way to measure our progress. I love the idea of men voluntarily giving up their male privilege—it would be great to figure out some means of measuring that stuff dropping by the wayside. But that's going to be a struggle—a struggle that's only going to be brought about by getting some more questions asked.

*King Lear, in the 1969 Brown University production of Shakespeare's **King Lear**, directed by James O. Barnhill. I'd like to do more Shakespeare—the women, or maybe the men.*

« 12 »

THE OTHER QUESTIONS

*Once I have restored Hollywood to its
ancient glory (and myself to what I was!), I
shall very simply restructure the human
race. This will entail the reduction of world
population through a complete change in
man's sexual image.*

—Gore Vidal, *Myron*, 1974

1. Where does Gender come from? Where does it keep coming from?

Is it really "natural?" What has gender got to do with penises, vaginas, chromosomes, or clothing? With hormones, lipstick, breasts, baldness, or beards?

Gender could be seen as a class system. By having gender around, there are these two classes—male and female. As in any binary, one side will always have more power than the other. One will always oppress the other. The value of a two-gender system is nothing more than the value of keeping the power imbalance, and all that depends on that, intact.

2. Can there be an equality between genders?

Or is "equality of the genders" oxymoronic, making any fight for the equality of the genders self-defeating? Gender implies class, and class presupposes inequality. Fight rather for the deconstruction of gender— it would get to the same place much faster.

But rather than look at some underlying reason for inequality, most people keep going on about the differences between the genders. The differences are only what we decide they are. And when some set of differences changes a little with time and with culture, we call those changes making progress in the area of gender, but gender is still there.

>> I'm nearly six feet tall, and I'm a big-boned gal. When I began living as a woman, men started opening doors for me, offering to carry packages, letting me go first down passageways. I was really puzzled. On the one hand, I was glad to be perceived as a woman; on the other hand, I didn't like being treated like a child.

>> But manners were only the beginning. I'd been in quite a few sales jobs—I knew how to sell...as a man. As a woman, the clients didn't want to hear my "expert opinion." As a woman, the clients wanted to hear me say, "Well, you know better than me, Mr. Jones—what do **you** think?"

>> As a man, I had access to work, and when I was out of work, I had very free access to job interviews. As a woman, for the first time in my life, I was told to not bother coming in for an interview.

>> The differences in the way men and women are **treated** are real. And the fact is this difference in treatment has no basis in the differences between men and women. I was the same person, and I was treated entirely differently. I got real interested in feminist theory—real fast.

There are differences enforced by the culture, and these need to be dealt with, but these differences are not intrinsic to the genders. By focusing on so-called "inherent differences" between men and women, we ignore and deny the existence of the gender system itself, and so we in fact hold it in place. But it's the gender system itself—the idea of gender itself—that needs to be done away with. The differences will then fall aside of their own accord.

I can see no other ethical basis for a recon-
ciliation [between men and women] than
the feminist principle—so often repeated—
that women are also persons, with the same
needs for respect, for satisfying work, for
love and pleasure—as men.
    —Barbara Ehrenreich, *The Hearts of*
Men: American Dreams and the Flight from
                        Commitment, 1984

3. Just how integral is gender to the culture?

Well, it's a patriarchal culture, and gender seems to be basic to the patriarchy. After all, men couldn't have male privilege if there were no males. And women couldn't be oppressed if there was no such thing as "women." Doing away with gender is key to the doing away with the patriarchy, as well as ending the many injustices perpetrated in the name of gender inequity. There is no gender inequity that doesn't first assume there is gender—and only two genders at that. Gender inequities include sexism, homophobia, and misogyny.

The struggle for women's rights (and to a lesser extent men's rights) is a vital stopgap measure until we do away with the system whose very nature maintains the imbalance and prohibits any harmony.

4. Is androgyny desirable or attainable?

Androgyny assumes that there's male stuff on one side of a spectrum, and female stuff on another side of that spectrum. And somewhere in the middle of this straight line, there's an ideal blend of "male" and "female." However, by saying there's a "middle," androgyny really keeps the opposites in place. By saying that we have a "male side" and a "female side," we blind ourselves to all the beautiful shades of identity of which we are each capable. Androgyny could be seen as a trap of the bi-polar gender system, as it further establishes the idea of two-and-only-two-genders.

Instead of imagining gender as opposite poles of a two-dimensional line, it would be interesting to twirl that line in space, and then spin it through several more dimensions. In this way, many more possibilities of gender identity may be explored.

> Exercise: Make a list of all the genders you observe in a week.
>
> Exercise: Make a list of all the genders you've been in a week.
>
> Exercise: Make a list of all the genders you can imagine in a week.

5. What is the source of gender's power?

Many cultures believe that names have power, and that by hiding one's name, one cannot be harmed. Calling someone or something by its real name strips it of its power.

> Names in general are very powerful, and most philosophies acknowledge that. The Old Testament says that the first act of humankind was to name things on the planet. The suit of Swords in the Tarot deck is the suit of naming, separating things out. (To this day, a sword is used in the naming ceremonies of English royalty.) But the suit of Swords (which became spades) is viewed as the suit of ruin, despair and bad luck—which is what you get, apparently, when you mess around with separating things out and naming them.

So, look for the oppression, and name it—give it some trouble; its name may well be gender. Please—don't call it "biological sex," or "social gender." Don't call it "sex" at all—sex is fucking, gender is everything else. Gender hides behind a great number of false names, and these names are all "types" of gender. But types of gender don't reveal anything about gender. Types of gender only reveal the paranoias of the societies that construct the types. Gender *becomes* typed in an attempt to hold together the boundaries of a given group. We can start doing away with gender by calling it gender.

6. How do people become gendered?

It depends on where you're sitting, but the system doesn't let you sit apart from gender for very long. The gender system of this culture fosters cult-like behavior. After all, membership in a gender is not based on informed consent. There is no possibility of abandoning membership without censure, ridicule, and danger. Members have no sense of humor regarding the cult of gender. Any humor that does exist about gender is based on the ridicule of its transgressors and non-members. Gender could use a good belly laugh at its own expense, but cults rarely get to laugh at themselves.

7. How does gender relate to identity?

Most of us assume that there *is* gender; that there are only two categories of gender, and that we are (have the identity of) one or the other. We have a lot invested in this belief—it's very difficult to imagine ourselves genderless. It's difficult to the degree that our identities are wrapped up in our gender assignments. We need to differentiate between having an identity and being an identity.

It's a fairly well-accepted principle that we seem to get into trouble when we define ourselves by things outside of ourselves. There are growing numbers of support groups dedicated to extricating their members from identity entanglements with one addiction or another—and these addictions are to things outside ourselves. There's trouble in defining ourselves by the food we eat, the drugs we take, or the kind of entertainment we like to indulge in. There's also trouble in defining ourselves by our race, our jobs, our relationships, our income level, our belongings, our age, our sexual orientation, our class, our politics, or our geography. All these things are transient, and when these things change—and change they do—we have identity crises.

> I mapped out the recurring pattern of the several identity crises I've experienced in my life: first I question an identity that I have, then I see all its bad qualities, and eventually I lose it or give it up. Then I get what seems to be a new, more pure, more unshakable identity, and I go through learning the ropes about what it means to be

that new identity. Then, once I'm comfortable in the new
identity, I question that, and the identity crisis starts all
over again. It's what I did with gender; it's what I'm still
doing with gender.

An identity crisis can occur around gender identity, except we usually don't notice it because we're so convinced that gender itself is
immutable and thereby immune to crisis. By defining ourselves as genderless, however, there's one less distraction to the development of our
own integrity. Please, assume no gender.

The 'third' is that which questions binary
thinking and introduces crisis.
  —Marjorie Garber, *Vested Interests*

8. What's a Transsexual?

Members of Transsexuality Anonymous in New York City made up
and distributed a button that said, "Take A Transsexual To Lunch." I
think that's particularly excellent advice. It may after all be *you* who's
the transsexual.

There's a myth in our culture that defines transsexuality as rare, and
transsexuals as oddities. But nearly everyone has some sort of bone to
pick with their own gender status, be it gender role, gender assignment,
or gender identity. And when this dissatisfaction can no longer be glossed
over with good manners, or cured by purchasing enough gender-specific products or services—and when this dissatisfaction cannot be silenced
by the authority of the state, the medical profession, the church, or one's
own peers—then the dissatisfaction is called transsexuality, or gender
dysphoria. We're most of us—whether "transsexual" or not—dissatisfied. Some of us have less tolerance for the dissatisfaction, that's all. I
accept the label transsexual as meaning only that I was dissatisfied with
my given gender, and I acted to change it. I am transsexual by choice,
not by pathology.

I'm called "gender dysphoric." That means I have a sickness: a limited understanding of gender. I don't think it's

that. I like to look at it that I **was** gender dysphoric for
my whole life before, and for some time after my gender
change—blindly buying into the gender system. As soon
as I came to some understanding about the constructed
nature of gender, and my relationship to that system, I
ceased being gender dysphoric.

People think they have to hate their genitals in order to be transsexual.
Well, some transsexuals do hate their genitals, and they act to change
them. But I think that transsexuals probably do not "naturally" hate
their birth-given genitals—I've not seen any evidence of that. We don't
hate any part of our bodies we weren't taught to hate. We're taught to
hate parts of our bodies that aren't "natural"—like a penis on a woman,
or a vagina on a man—and it seems that the arbiters of nature are the
doctors.

Transsexuality is a medicalized phenomenon. The term was invented
by a doctor. The system is perpetuated by doctors. But the demedicalization of transsexualism is a dilemma. There is a demand for genital
surgery, largely as a result of the cultural genital imperative. Due to
financial requirements, the fulfillment of the surgical dream is subject
to cultural and class constraints; cosmetic and genital conversion surgery
is available primarily to the middle and upper classes. Transsexuals,
especially middle-class pre-operative transsexuals, are heavily invested
in maintaining their status as "diseased" people. The demedicalization of
transsexuality would further limit surgery in this culture, as it would
remove the label of "illness" and so prohibit insurance companies from
footing the bill.

I had my genital surgery partially as a result of cultural
pressure: I couldn't be a "real woman" as long as I had a
penis. Knowing what I know now, I'm real glad I had my
surgery, and I'd do it again, just for the comfort I now
feel with a constructed vagina. I **like** that thang!

Loren Cameron puts forward the theory that there is a continuum of
managing one's gender. For some people, comfort is only achieved

through genital surgery; for others, an occasional evening of dress-up suffices just fine. Each of us needs to name and attain our own point of comfort. Insurance-based coverage for genital surgery should, I believe, be made available for those who can't afford it, and for whom the comfort point would require that surgery.

To some transsexuals, the state of transsexuality itself is seen as transitory—a cocoon. In goes one gender, out comes the other. So there's a pre-change and post-change transsexual. Through it's insistence and fierce maintenance of the man/woman dichotomy, the culture puts the pre-change transsexual in the position of needing to say a permanent good-bye to one gender, and then and only then say hello to another. While that good-bye/hello is certainly an option, this culture is making it the *only* option. A viable solution to such a "choice" is to disentangle oneself long enough from the culture or individual presenting the two alternatives, so that you can explore some other options.

Anne Bolin describes the pre-change transsexual's journey in terms of an anthropological model: the pre-change individual withdraws from the culture, its rules and its company, in order to effect the loss of one identity and the taking-on of another. That new identity firmly in place, the post-change individual then re-enters the culture. The process is nearly identical to the breakup of a relationship, with the transgendered person leaving behind one gender in order to assume another.

> Negative definitions of partner and relationship precede and accompany the leavetaking because the loss must be turned into an acceptable loss. We justify our failure to ourselves by dwelling on the negative aspects of what we are leaving behind.
> —Diane Vaughan, *Uncoupling: How Relationships Come Apart*, 1987

It's the old story of devaluing the outsider, only in this case, the outsider is the gender one is taking leave of. By devaluing the gender left behind, the transsexual perpetuates the "war" between the genders.

But now there's a new generation of transsexuals who are assessing their journey not as either/or, but rather as an integration, a whole. In bypassing the either/or construct of what has up to now been transsexualism, these new transsexuals are slipping out from under the control of the culture. And a new sub-culture is being born.

Many people divide transsexuals into pre-operative and post-operative, referring to genital conversion surgery. I want to include the option of a "non-operative" transsexual—someone who doesn't opt for the genital surgery.

> One answer to the question "Who is a transsexual?" might well be "Anyone who admits it." A more political answer might be, "Anyone whose performance of gender calls into question the construct of gender itself."

Admitting it is so difficult. The dynamic of transsexualism today is the dynamic of an oppressed people faced with no alternative to forced assimilation into a culture that would rather see them dead. The response to this oppression is the rise of individual transsexuals who resist this. The successful methods by which the resistance will occur is unpredictable, even to the gender rebels themselves.

9. How does gender relate to power?

Power seems basic to gender, and gets played out *through* gender, usually without the permission or even the understanding of the people involved in the playing.

To change [gender] is to slide along a power differential. To change power is to change [gender].
    —Marjorie Garber, *Vested Interests*

The current gender system relies heavily on everyone's agreement that it's inflexible. Key to the doing away with gender is the ability to freely move into and out of existing genders and gender roles. Like butch and femme. Like top and bottom. And eventually, like man and woman. Sadomasochism (S/M) can be a consensual way to play with power and gender through sex.

There are several definitions for sadomasochism. One is used by the puritanical wing of the S/M debate, the other by the practitioners themselves. The former see sadomasochism as non-consensual violence, rape, and other forms of unspeakable cruelty and oppression. Most practitioners, and I'm one, see S/M in terms of a loving consensual act. One (or more) person is top, or dominant; one (or more) person is bottom, or submissive. In many cases, S/M players negotiate their needs, their wants, their fantasies and restrictions (medical, emotional, psychological, etc.) prior to any actual playing.

"Playing" is one term commonly used to describe S/M sexual activities. Those who are playing have agreed upon their roles, and the boundaries within which they will play. In most scenarios, there are ways to end the play or exit the scene safely and quickly if it's becoming too much for one or more of the players. Discussions abound within the S/M community about who holds the power in an S/M game: the top or the bottom. Most players agree that power is *shared*, with the top in control but only within the bounds agreed upon and often requested by the bottom. Some say there's a sublime moment when top and bottom together and at once have all the power and none of the power.

S/M play can accommodate any combinations of sex, power, and gender play. When the play reaches the point of almost purely dealing with power, then many S/M players agree that gender has in fact been done away with.

> This could possibly contribute to the current taboos placed on S/M by leaders of some branches of feminism, as well as by the more vocally conservative patriarchy: they're both too invested in maintaining their genders and the gender system which defines their own boundaries, self-definitions, and ideologies.

The Outcasts, a San Francisco-based women's S/M organization, define three keys to sadomasochistic play: S/M must be safe, sane, and consensual—by playing this way, S/M uncovers the hidden power games of the culture. Safe, sane, and consensual sadomasochism necessitates *talking* about these games. On a day-to-day basis, we may get caught up in some cultural power games without wanting to get so entangled. In S/M, we *play* at these power games because the playing is fun. Similarly, we can play at gender precisely because it is fun.

I was asked recently to talk at an Outcasts meeting about gender play and S/M play:

> I think gender can take a lesson from S/M: gender needs to be safe, sane, and consensual.
>
> Gender is not safe.
> If I change my gender, I'm at risk of homicide, suicide or a life devoid of half my possibilities.
> If I'm born with a body that gives mixed gender signals, I'm at risk of being butchered—fixed, mutilated.
> Gender is not safe.
>
> And gender is not sane.
> It's not sane to call a rainbow black and white.
> It's not sane to demand we fit into one or the other only.
> It's not sane that we classify people in order to oppress them as women or to glorify them as men.
> Gender is not sane.
>
> And gender is not consensual.
> We're born: a doctor assigns us a gender. It's documented by the state, enforced by the legal profession, sanctified by the church, and it's bought and sold in the media.
> We have no say in our gender—we're not allowed to question it, play with it, work it out with our friends, lovers, or family.
> Gender is not consensual.
>
> Safe gender is being who and what we want to be when we want to be that, with no threat of censure or violence.
> Safe gender is going as far in any direction as we wish,

with no threat to our health, or to anyone else's.
Safe gender is not being pressured into passing, not having to lie, not having to hide.

Sane gender is asking questions about gender—talking
to people who do gender, and opening up about our gender histories and our gender desires.
Sane gender is probably very, very funny.

Consensual gender is respecting each others' definitions
of gender, and respecting the wishes of some to be alone,
and respecting the intentions of others to be inclusive in
their own time.
Consensual gender is non-violent in that it doesn't force
its way in on anyone.
Consensual gender opens its arms and welcomes all people as gender outcasts—whoever is willing to admit to it.

Gender has a lot to learn from S/M.
And we who know S/M are a lot further along the road to
safe, sane, consensual gender play than we may realize.
We just need to apply the basics.

—from a talk at the April 1993 Outcasts meeting

If living gender-free can shine a light on personal identity, then living
with S/M can illuminate inter-personal dynamics. S/M as a sexual
preference is an alternative to the gay/straight dichotomy served up in
this culture.

Sadomasochism intersects gender at the point of performance. We
perform our identities, which include gender, and we perform our relationships, which include sex. Transgender is simply identity more consciously performed on the infrequently used playing field of gender.
S/M is simply a relationship more consciously performed within the
forbidden arena of power.

S/M partners play at what the culture often refuses to acknowledge about itself—owning or belonging to one other. This game highlights factors basic to power: the need to belong, and its two corollaries: the need to own and the need to exclude. We rarely think about the concept of belonging to something as "being owned" by something, but that's what it means. This culture teaches us to belong to one gender or another, in the same way that we're taught we need to *own* a home, *belong* to a nuclear family, *have* a profession, *occupy* a geographical location, and let's not forget we need a place to call our *own*.

Our culture also tells us that we are what we belong to. To give up membership is to give up identity, and while that's not ultimately harmful, it is frightening. In the same way we unlearn other outmoded and/or harmful cultural imperatives, we need to unlearn gender. In the same way we need to break free of systems that enslave us, we need to break free of gender. The fear and hatred of gender outlaws and S/M players is the fear and hatred of those who do not belong, who aren't owned lock, stock, and barrel by the gender system.

10.   Why is there so much emphasis on passing?

Passing is a form of pretending, which can be fun. In gender, passing is currently defined as the act of appearing in the world as a gender to which one does not belong, or as a gender to which one did not formerly belong. Most passing is undertaken in response to the cultural imperative to be one gender or the other. In this case, passing becomes the outward manifestation of shame and capitulation. Passing becomes silence. Passing becomes invisibility. Passing becomes lies. Passing becomes self-denial.

A more universal and less depressing definition of passing would be the act of appearing in the gender of one's choice. Everyone is passing; some have an easier job of it than others.

> There's a reward and punishment mechanism to passing. As much as I go on about this stuff, and as out of the closet as I am on a very broad public level, I still make an effort to walk down the street and pass on a very private level. I do this because I don't want to get beaten up. I do this because all my life it's been something I've wanted—to live as a

> woman—and by walking through the world looking like
> one, I have that last handhold on the illusion, the fantasy,
> the dream of it all. Passing is seductive—people don't look
> at you like you're some kind of freak.

On the punishment side of the coin, there's a deep shame involved in any failure to pass. As I was preparing the final draft of this book, someone I know only peripherally came over to my house on an errand—he was with an ex-lover of mine. In casual conversation, he slipped on a pronoun and referred to me as "he."

Let me tell you what happened, the way it looked from inside my head. The world slowed down, like it does in the movies when someone is getting shot and the filmmaker wants you to feel every bullet enter your body. The words echoed in my ears over and over and over. Attached to that simple pronoun was the word *failure*, quickly followed by the word *freak*. All the joy sucked out of my life in that instant, and every moment I'd ever fucked up crashed down on my head. Here was someone who'd never known me as a man, referring to me as a man. Instead of saying or doing anything, I shut down and was polite to him for the rest of the time he was in my house.

Now here's a telling point: all three of us (as I later found out) were aware of that slip, and none of us said anything. *He's* a trained sex worker, with a great deal of experience working with sexual and gender minorities. *She* had two transsexual lovers, me having been one of them. I'm a transsexual. We all knew he'd slipped on a pronoun, and none of us said anything—not a giggle, not an "oops," not one comment. Each of us was far too embarrassed to say anything 'til the next day. What does that say about the gender imperative? I think it says everything.

> Who reads us? People whose identity hinges on the need
> to determine gender: gays and lesbians for sexual rea-
> sons, sex workers and street people for economic reasons,
> children for the reason of trying to establish their own
> place in the system.

Passing emphatically equals membership, and passing includes all the privileges of gender membership. There is most certainly a privilege to having a gender. Just ask someone who doesn't have a gender, or who can't pass, or who doesn't pass. When you have a gender, or when you are perceived as having a gender, you don't get laughed at in the street. You don't get beat up. You know which public bathroom to use, and when you use it, people don't stare at you or worse. You know which form to fill out. You know what clothes to wear. You have heroes and role models. You have a past.

Passing by choice can be fantastic fun. Enforced passing is a joyless activity. Any joy that might be generated by the passing cannot be shared. Similarly, the joy of history lies in its telling and in its relevance to current times and relationships. Transgendered people, particularly post-operative transsexuals, are not allowed any history beyond their current gender—we're not supposed to reveal our transgender status or our other-gendered past. Denied the opportunity to speak our stories, transsexuals are denied the joy of our histories. Sometimes it's painful for me to recall having been male: I did some stupid stuff—but that's part of me, and I need my male past as a reference point in my life. Discouraged from examining our past, transgendered people are discouraged from growth.

> The biggest gift for me after having gone through my gender change was getting back in touch with people I'd known when I was a guy. I really thought I'd never hear from them again. I thought they'd all think I was too weird to be in touch with. One by one, as I get back in touch with folks from my past, I can measure the continuity of my life. And I'm so grateful for their open minds and their open hearts.

The concept of passing is built into the culture's definition of transsexuality; and the result is that transsexuals don't question the gender system which their very existence could topple. Instead, through the mandate of passing, the culture uses transsexuals to reinforce the bipolar gender system, as transsexuals strive for recognition within their new gender, and thus the privilege and chains of their new gender.

Ironically, the concept of passing invites and even demands the concept of reading (seeing through someone else's attempt at passing) and being read. The culture desires and will insist upon an unmasking; the culture will have its "truth." The fear of being read as transsexual weighs so heavily on an individual that it focuses even more attention on "passing." It's a conundrum, because more and better passing brings about an increased fear of being read. I know too many transsexuals who deny their lives as transsexual for the sake of appearing "normal."

11.   What about the cultural exploitation of transgendered people?
I think it's inevitable, I think it's not unique to transgendered people, and I think it will only continue to the degree we allow it to continue. Most minorities have been exoticized by some dominant culture. A dominant culture, to be truly dominant, needs freak populations—be they racial, religious, and gender minorities, or whatever. True exploitation involves the appropriation of the minority's voice.

In the nineteenth century, one venue for the exoticization of minorities was the North American traveling medicine show. It worked like this: the manager of the show wanted to make money by selling some goods. This manager would gather up a group of exotics—usually people of non-white races, or people with physical anomalies (including hermaphrodites)—publicize the attributes of these "freaks," and then charge admission for the general public to come into some tent to look at them. Then the barker would launch into a talk about the exhibited minority person, or freak. The freak would say nothing, or would recite some rehearsed speech approved by the barker, who had a stake in maintaining the dehumanization of the freak so he could charge more money. The barker would proceed to sell his goods, making a double nickel from the attendees.

In this century, there's a similar venue: the television talk show. The barker, or host, still parades the freaks out in front of the audience, but here's the big difference: it's the *sponsor* who sells the goods during the commercial break. The division of labor between barker-as-host and salesperson-as-sponsor has allowed for a whole new window of opportunity for the freak. Because the TV talk show host (barker) is not the person *directly* interested in sales, he or she can afford to be somewhat more interested in the guests (freaks). The talk show host has a stake in a ratings number, not the number of bottles of snake oil sold, so the host/barker can afford to be more sensitive and caring about the guests/freaks. The good television talk show host realizes that he or she has a stake in emphasizing the *humanity* of the guests so that the viewing audience can better identify with them. As a result, the freaks have an opportunity to speak their own words—for the first time, and to a broad audience! In this culture, I'm a freak—that's why I respect and enjoy doing the talk shows.

> I love freaks. I really do. I always have.
>
> When I was a young boy, my father took me to the circus. I don't remember anything about the circus performance. All I remember is the sideshow. And what I remember most is Olaf, the world's tallest man. He was so tall, I had to stretch my neck way back in order to see all of him. He wore a brown suit. I remember that part. His feet were as long as my arm. He was quiet. He had...dignity. But, his hands —damn, his hands were enormous. On each of his fingers, he wore rings, which he sold as souvenirs. I remember I was standing up front, close to his stage, as he spoke of his life. I didn't understand a word he said, but I worshipped him. And then he bent down toward me. His already immense head grew larger and larger as his face drew near to mine. And I remember no fear. He knew me, and I knew him. He smiled. I smiled. Then he took one of the rings off his finger, and put it round my wrist. And I knew I was just like him. I knew I was a freak.
>
> Freaks always know that.

I love doing television talk shows—I respect the format. I'm a child of television, so I'm familiar with the venue, and I've learned the language of sound-bytes. I know now to prepare ahead of time the point I want to get across, so I don't have to think on my feet. Unlike Olaf, I don't need some barker to approve my material before I present it. I can have fun bantering with the host, and parrying questions and answers with the audience. And I can usually get back to the single point I want to make on that show.

> When a politician appears on a talk show, he's called media-savvy. When I appear on a talk show, I'm called self-centered, self-serving, and a freak. Go figure.

There's a comfortable, three-way symbiosis among the talk show hosts, their guests, and their audiences. The relationship between host and guest is a tacit understanding of the need to communicate to the largest possible number of viewers, and to fulfill some "social service" obligation of information dissemination. It's theater, and both host and guest play a role, one in agreement with the other. The relationship between the two of them and the audience is more magical—like the magic between a young child and a circus giant.

But the real cultural exploitation of transgendered people today is evident in comedy skits like "It's Pat," (recently rumored to soon be a major motion picture). When I first heard about the skit, I thought it was a great idea, but I figured the joke would be on all the characters who were desperate to determine Pat's gender. Instead, the joke was consistently on Pat, who is shown as a slobbering, unattractive, simpering nerd. Pat, of course, *cannot* be attractive, because that would return gender ambiguity to its apparently rightful place of being desirable, and that's simply too dangerous. The popularity of this skit is pretty clear evidence that transgendered people are considered fair game for cultural scapegoating. We're still the group that wears no sign proclaiming, "To fuck with me is politically incorrect and social suicide, so hands off." There's no civil rights group to come to Pat's defense or to the defense of those in Pat's position outside the tube. "It's Pat" is the latest installment in a sadly long tradition of comedy that objectifies, vilifies, and dehumanizes an otherwise voiceless minority.

12.   Is there a role for the transgendered in this culture?
I don't believe it's up to the culture to create such a role. I think it's up to the transgendered to claim one for themselves.

Our culture, some say, has no place for the transgendered. There are some who point to other cultures with envy. These other cultures, they say, have established roles for the transgendered. Hijras in India, for example, call themselves "neither men nor women." Their role in Indian culture is a spiritual one, presiding over marriages and births. Yet as India becomes increasingly westernized, the Hijras are being systematically wiped out.

Whereas Westerners feel uncomfortable with the ambiguities and contradictions inherent in such in-between categories as transvestism, homosexuality, hermaphroditism, and transgenderism, and make strenuous attempts to resolve them, Hinduism not only accommodates such ambiguities, but also views them as meaningful and even powerful.
— Serena Nanda, *Neither Men Nor Women: The Hijras of India*, 1990

Our Western culture has no room for any shades of grey, so it wouldn't make much sense to expect this bi-polar culture to create a role for people whose very existence threatens the binary. The transgendered shamans of other cultures earned their roles; their roles as guides and healers were not doled out to them. Similarly, today's transgendered must earn a position in today's culture. That place in the world will certainly not be a gift to us. Left to fate, the roles we have been gifted with in today's culture have been roles of shame and death.

It would be important that any role that the transgendered wind up claiming is not a role that would by its very existence forward the culture that oppresses the transgendered and related border-walkers.

>> Any us-versus-them position forwards a culture that oppresses the transgendered. Opt rather for a role that is inclusive, and promotes inclusion.
>> Any position which operates non-consensually (violently) forwards a culture that oppresses the transgen-

> dered. Choose only positions which trade in mutual
> agreement.
>
> ›› Any power-over position forwards a culture that
> oppresses the transgendered. We should look for posi-
> tions that allow us to bring out the power we have
> within us, and to acknowledge the power of others.

13.   You say you want a revolution?

Over the past decade, transgendered people have increasingly been
speaking in their own voice. It's the beginnings of a revolution.

> The problem with revolution, of course, is violence. It
> would be neat to take part in a non-violent revolution of
> inclusion, whereby the revolutionaries simply have a good
> laugh, and welcome anyone else to dinner.

Guess Who's Coming to the Revolution?

In defining the left and right wings of the gender discourse, one need
only look at who has an investment in the bi-polar gender system for
the sake of their identity. Any revolution in deconstructing gender
should look for *no* support among communities of people whose identities depend on the existence of this bi-polar gender system. This would
include, but most certainly is not limited to, the fundamentalist right
wing, purists in the lesbian and gay male communities who believe in
the ultimate goal of assimilation into the dominant culture, and some
cultural or radical feminists. Non-supporters of any movement to
deconstruct gender would also, unfortunately, include those transgendered people who subscribe fully to the culture's definitions of gender,
and seek to embody those definitions within themselves. It's the agreement with the dominant culture that keeps people believing in this gender system: straight or gay has nothing to do with it.

> Judeo-Christian fundamentalists, radical lesbian sepa-
> ratists, and the more vocal transgender activists all seem
> to be united against the theory that you don't **have** to

be a man or a woman. I wanted to find out what they
have in common. When I looked deeper than their common need for a fixed gender, it hit me that we're talking
an old, old philosophical conflict here: we're talking
order versus chaos—some people need one or the other.
In our postmodern global village, order and chaos could
very well be used to define the real right wing (order)
and left wing (chaos) of any discourse.

Straights and gays alike demand the need for an orderly gender system:
they're two sides of the same coin, each holding the other in place, neither willing to dismantle the gender system that serves as a matrix for
their (sexual) identity. Because of the bi-polar nature of both sexual orientation and gender, one system strengthens the other. Bisexuality and
androgyny also hold two sides in place by defining themselves as somewhere in the middle of two given polar opposites.

Deikman maintains that it is important to devalue those outside the
group. In terms of marginal queer culture, the irony is all too clear.
Lesbians, gay men, and other queer people first burst into the world as
self-defined outlaws. "We are not like you," they said to the heterosexual culture. Today, many former outlaws paradoxically wish to exist
within the very culture that defines us as outsiders, and this is the
beginning of assimilationism.

In order to reinforce their newly-included position within the dominant ideology, assimilationist lesbians, gays, bisexuals, and transgendered people must accept the rules and the boundaries of the straight
culture. They need to cast as outsiders those who would threaten the
integrity of their membership. They need to disown their own.

It's no surprise that the steering committee for the 1993
March on Washington for Lesbian, Gay, and Bi Rights—the
largest-ever civil rights march in the U.S.—voted to
exclude the word "transgender" from the title of the march.

Supporters of a movement to deconstruct gender might be found within
groups of people who are looking beyond gender for identity—some

more liberal or radical segments of the S/M and bisexual communities, for example, or radical queer elements who want to do away with the rigid codes of gender and sexuality. It's the people who would give gender deconstruction a bad name who would probably work the hardest for it. It's the people who would lend "respectability" to the notion who would never work towards it.

Who Are the Allies?

Transgendered people are mistakenly viewed as the cusp of the lesbian and gay community. In reality the two huge communities are like circles that only partially overlap.
—Leslie Feinberg, *Transgender Liberation: A Movement Whose Time Has Come*, 1992

If we're going to work with one another to achieve rights for all, then we need to include one another in our struggles. So who gets to include whom becomes a pressing question.

The lesbian and gay community is solidifying and becoming more of a codified group—existing within and accepted by the dominant ideology. Self-defined "Queers" become more and more the adversarial outsiders, the ungrateful children, the bad influence—queers like the drag queens, the stone butches, the dyke leather daddies, the she-males—the ones who are going to "wreck everything" for (assimilated) lesbian and gays.

Assuming that gay men and lesbians are more consciously excluded by the culture for violations of *gender* codes (which are visible in the daily life of the culture) than for actual sexual practices (which usually happen behind closed doors and in private spaces), then lesbians and gay men actually share the same stigma with "transgendered" people: the stigma of crimes against gender. And while "transgendered" people may not in fact practice gay or lesbian sex, and so may not themselves be lesbian or gay, gays and lesbians are invariably perceived as "transgendered."

So let's reclaim the word "transgendered" so as to be more inclusive.

Let's let it mean "transgressively gendered." Then, we have a group of people who break the rules, codes, and shackles of gender. Then we have a healthy-sized contingent! It's the transgendered who need to embrace the lesbians and gays, because it's the transgendered who are in fact the more inclusive category.

Of course, this will offend everyone. It will seem to negate and belittle the hard-won gains of lesbians and gay men. It will tend to make invisible the bisexuals. It will seem to dilute a supposedly unique transgender struggle. But it's the only point all these groups have in common, it's the only flag around which they all could rally. Failing one great big happy family under one great big happy name, we need to at least stop attacking each other.

It's going to be difficult. For lesbians and gays to include transgendered people, or indeed be included by them, it would require that gays and lesbians admit to what amounts to their own transgender status. It would require that they question their definition of their sexual identity, which is currently based solely on the gender of their desired partners. That's a lot to ask, but I think that competent and compassionate negotiators from the sexual and gender minority camps could get together and come up with some umbrella name that would be more inclusive, and acceptable to the majority. Lesbians and gay men today stand at a crossroads with bisexuals and transgendered people, says Leslie Feinberg. Further down the road, we're going to need all the community we can muster when it comes time to stand at the crossroads against patriarchal oppression. Only our bonding will permit a true revolution of sex and gender.

14.   Where's the fun?

All roads in life lead nowhere. So, you might
as well take the road that has the most
heart and is the most fun.

                        —Anonymous Zen saying

It's frightening to be genderless. What makes it easier is a sense of humor, and that's where camp comes into the picture. Camp is a uniquely queer experience. It's a sense of humor developed in response to oppression based on a unique gender identity, and a minority sexual orientation.

*It is possible to discern strong themes in any particular campy thing or event. The three that seemed most recurrent and characteristic to me were **incongruity**, **theatricality**, and **humor**. All three are intimately related to the homosexual situation and strategy. Incongruity is the subject matter of camp, theatricality its style, and humor its strategy.*
—Esther Newton, *Mother Camp: Female Impersonators in America*, 1972

Camp thumbs its nose at the straight world, lampooning and violating its rituals. Camp points out the silliness, exaggerates the roles, shines big spotlights on the gender dynamic. Camp is only possible when there is no fear of humiliation and at that point, social control becomes very difficult.

As theater, the Sisters of Perpetual Indulgence are electric. They cannot be ignored. The minute they appear on the scene, the atmosphere is charged with humor, hostility, disgust—but rarely indifference.
—Kevin Starr, *"Indulging the Sisters," The San Francisco Examiner*, 1981

When we think of camp, we usually think of a man in a dress, but men aren't the only ones who lampoon the culture's definition of women and men. Performers like Dominique Dibell, member of The Five Lesbian Brothers, take both girl and boy drag onto the stage.

I enjoy doing feminine drag—female drag. It was a great revolution when femmes started to come out and say that we could embrace

this way of looking—this femme role—and
be powerful and sexy and attractive to
women; and still be 100% lesbian. That's
always exciting for me to see and to per-
form. The <u>male</u> drag thing has always been a
traditionally lesbian thrill, and it still is.
Male drag is very sexy, and that's what it's
about. There's just something about putting
a masculine wrapper on a female body—you
just want to take the wrapper off!
  —Dominique Dibell, personal interview
            with the author, 1993

Some folks think that camp, or drag in general, is an attempt to ape or become the dominant culture. What I learned to see once I got off the straight and narrow road was this: camp performers were taking pieces of the culture and twisting them around to a point of humor and then and only then wearing the scalps (wigs) of their oppressors as badges of victory.

> High camp can be a man in full nun drag, with great
> showgirl make-up, on roller-skates in the middle of town.
> Does that man really want to be a nun?

Camp has always been with us. It's had other names in other times; and other leanings in other cultures. In India, for example, there exists an old tradition of jesters, *Bhands*, or *bahurupiya*. Their function in the Rajasthan caste society seems quite similar to the function of camp performers in today's Eurocentric culture.

As a joker in the deck, a "wild card" in an
otherwise carefully labeled pack, the
bahurupiya *serves as a reminder that*
even in the most rigid societies, identities
are not fixed. The wheel of karma takes
many turns; a prince in one cycle may find

*himself a pauper in another as the **lila**—*
or play—of life continues.
    —John Emigh, "Hajari Bhand: A Joker in
        the Deck," *The Drama Review*, 1986

Camp can be a leading edge in the deconstruction of gender, because camp wrests social control from the hands of the fanatics. Camp in fact reclaims gender and re-shapes it as a consensual game. Setting about to do away with gender could itself turn into a frighteningly fanatical mission. Fanatics are distinguishable by the fact that they can't laugh at themselves. Camp is the safety valve that can keep any gender activism from becoming fanaticism.

In doing away with a bi-polar gender system, one needn't do away with playing at genders. Drag is fun! Cultural drag queens like Madonna and Arnold Schwarzenegger are opening doors for all of us. Arnold Schwarzenegger does male drag perfectly, only he doesn't seem to have much of a sense of humor about it yet. His next movie will probably have him in the woods—drumming and chanting.

15.   What about the future of gender?

I think it's already here today, alive and thriving within the structures of our primitive virtual realities. Although the term conjures up visions of goggles and gloves electronically linked to a computer, I like a broader definition of virtual reality, which would embrace the written word, the telephone, electronic bulletin boards, and the great, grand ancestor of all virtual realities, theater.

Theater is [Brenda] Laurel's metaphor for virtual reality. In a field with almost no historical perspective, she draws on thousands of years of theatrical analysis. To Laurel, the V[irtual] R[eality] user is an actor, playing off other actors, taking action, exploring characters, experimenting with appearances, behavior, or gender. "Reality has always been too small for the human imagination. We're

always trying to transcend," Laurel says.
  —Susan McCarthy, "Techno-soaps and
      Virtual Theater," Wired, 1993

Gender is a method of partitioning our identities, our families, our economics, or our society. Virtual Reality is a method of making partitions obsolete. We have the opportunity to play with gender in much the same way that we get to play with other forms of identity—through performance in any virtual medium. In any medium, there have always been cross-gendered performances.

> When I was a phone sex hostess, I knew quite a few hostesses who were men. The actual gender of the hostesses didn't matter, as long as they could act. Phone sex was theater. The hostesses were playing their roles, for which they'd get paid, and the clients played their roles, for which opportunity they'd pay us.

More sophisticated virtual realities allow for more opportunities to play with gender, as well as more sophisticated methods of playing, but any virtual reality is a playing field on which we can rehearse for the future.

> On some of the "pay for play" public electronic bulletin boards, like **America Online**, **Prodigy**, or **Compuserve**, there can always be found men who are on-line as women. Similarly, I've known a few women who've gone on-line as men.
>
> I've gone on-line as straight women, bisexual women, and lesbian women. I haven't given much thought to going on-line as a man—I've had all the male experience I'd like, thank you very much.

The futures of gender, spirituality, and virtual reality all converge at the horizon line of the millennium. If we begin, in virtual reality, to render partitions as needless, or at best as boundaries for some consensual game, then we have the opportunity to carry that skill over into our day-to-day worlds.

Now What?

Having asked some questions, it's time to explore the possibilities that the questions have raised. Any theory is only meaningful if it can be put to use, and it should be possible to apply these principles in a more or less measurable arena. Fortunately, gender is so pervasive in the culture that there are an infinite number of circumstances for playing with it, and, after raising the questions, it will be the act of playing with gender that's going to change cultural attitudes about gender.

We bring about the future of gender when we put gender into play in any aspect of our daily lives: family, work, play, or relationship. It's when we put gender into play, it's when we question the binary, it's when we break the rules and keep calling attention to the fact that the rules are breakable: that's when we create a Third Space. I've been putting gender to play in theater, and it was through theater that I discovered how to apply this theory. My queer theater was my Third Space.

Yearbook Photo, 1969.

creating a third space

I think it's up to each transgressively gendered person to create a space for this life as
Third. At home, at play, and at work. My
workplace is the theater, and while there is
a lot of theater about folks like us, there is
very little space for us in person. Like other
transgressively gendered folks, I'm managing
to get a foot in the door; my door is the Stage
Door, that's all.

On the **Geraldo** segment, "Transsexual Regrets: Who's Sorry Now?" I was the one who **wasn't** sorry.

« 13 »

TRANSSEXUAL LESBIAN
PLAYWRIGHT TELLS ALL!

*Written as a talk for the Out/Write '90 conference
of lesbian and gay writers, in San Francisco and
adapted for inclusion in the anthology* **High Risk**.

My ancestors were performers. In life. The earliest shamanic rituals involved women and men exchanging genders. Old, old rituals. Top-notch performances. Life and death stuff. We're talking cross-cultural here. We're talking rising way way way above being a man or a woman. That's how my ancestors would fly. That's how my ancestors would talk with the goddesses and the gods. Old rituals.

I'd been a performer of one sort or another for over twenty-five years, and now I'm writing plays as well as performing in them. See, I had never seen my story on stage and I was looking. I used to go up to writers I knew. I used to wish they'd write my story. And I'm only just now realizing that they couldn't possibly. I write from the point of view of an *S/M* transsexual lesbian, ex-cult member, femme top and some-times bottom shaman. And I wondered why no one was writing my story? I'm writing from the point of view of used-to-be-a-man, three husbands, father, first mate on an ocean-going yacht, minister, high-powered IBM sales type, Pierre Cardin three-piece suitor, bar-mitz-vah'd, circumcised yuppie from the East Coast. Not too many women write from that point of view. I write from the point of view of a used-to-be politically correct, wanna-be butch, dyke phone sex hostess, smooth talking, telemarketing, love slave, art slut, pagan Tarot reader, maybe soon a grandmother, crystal palming, incense burning, not-man, not always a woman, fast becoming a Marxist. And not too many men write from that point of view.

My ancestors didn't write much. I guess they didn't need to.

Y'know, people try to write about transsexuals and it's amusing it's infuriating it's patronizing and it's why *I'm* writing about transsexuals now. I wrote one play in college twenty-one years ago. And one play last year. Both of them I pulled from my chest until they pulsed bleeding on the stage. Saint Kate of the bleeding heart. The first play was young love gone bad. Spun out my soul as just so much cotton candy romanticism. God it felt great. The second play was a harder birth. *Hidden: A Gender* is my transsexual voice—the voice I speak with, cry with, roar with, moan with and laugh with, don't forget laugh with. I always hid that voice away. I always used your voice, spoke your words, sang your hit parade. Until I heard them whisper, my ancestors. And I whispered and you heard me and I said hey you weren't meant to hear that and you said tell us more. And that was the second play, the harder birth. The one I had to write.

I write when nothing else will bring me peace, when I burn, when I find myself asking and answering the same questions over and over. I write when I've begun to lose my sense of humor and it becomes a matter of my life and my death to get that sense of humor back and watch you laugh. I write in bottom space. I open up to you, I cut myself, I show you my fantasies, I get a kick out of that—oh, yeah. I perform in top space. I cover myself with my character and take you where you never dreamed you could go. Yes. My ancestors did this. My instrument is not my pen or my typewriter, not my lover's Macintosh, not my cast of characters, not my body on stage. No, my instrument is my audience and oh how I love to play you.

And to what end? I've come to see gender as a divisive social construct, and the gendered body as a somewhat dubious accomplishment. I write about this because I am a gender outlaw and my issues are gender issues. The way I see it now, the lesbian and gay community is as much oppressed for gender transgressions as for sexual distinction. We have more in common, you and I, than most people are willing to admit. See,

I'm told I must be a man or a woman. One or the other. Oh, it's OK to be a transsexual say some—just don't talk about it. Don't question your gender any more, just be a woman now—you went to so much trouble—just be satisfied. I am so, not satisfied. My ancestors were not satisfied.

I write from the point of view of a gender outlaw because I don't want to hear: We don't want you in our club / We don't want you on our land / We don't want you in our march. And I say I don't know why the separatists won't let me in—I'm *probably* the only lesbian to have successfully castrated a man and gone on to laugh about it on stage, in print, and on national television.

Hello, Geraldo, are you reading this?

My ancestors were not shunned. They were celebrated. Look, I know you try to fill in the blanks in my life. I write to let you know who I am so that you *can* fill in the blanks.

Hello, Mom, are you reading this?

Anyway, I work in theater because I really enjoy working *with* people, and theater is not an alone art. And current theatrical forms reflect a rigidly bi-polar gender system. They aren't fluid enough for what I want to say, and I feel that form and content in theater as in life should be complementary, not adversarial, so I work on my own gender fluidity and sometimes it works and sometimes it doesn't. And I work on the fluidity of my theatrical style—and sometimes it works and sometimes it doesn't. My life and my theater—my form and my content—sort of do as I say and do as I do. Like my ancestors.

—San Francisco, March 1990

*Promotional photo for the first production of **Hidden: A Gender**, directed by Noreen C. Barnes. (top to bottom) Kate Bornstein, Sydney Erskine, Justin Bond.*

« 14 »

QUEER LIFE / QUEER THEATER

I see theater as the performance of identity, which is acknowledged as a performance. We're always performing identities, but when we *consciously* perform one, and people *acknowledge* our performance, it's theater. When people hone the skill of that performance to a point where other people will actually pay to see them do it, the skilled people are called actors or performers or theater artists, and they can charge admission.

The two things I thought I'd have to give up by going through my gender change were orgasms and theater.

See, my surgeon warned me that I might have no more sensation in my genitals after surgery—that I may never have another orgasm.

My own insecurity insisted that I'd never be able to perform on stage again. I mean, who would ever cast me? What kind of role could I play? There were few enough parts for women—but a woman like me? I was a freak, and there was no place for me in the theater I'd grown up with and trained in. I went through my gender change anyway—a stable gender identity mattered that much more at the time.

As it turned out, I never got a stable gender identity. I did end up, however, with both orgasms and theater.

As individuals express their life, so they are.
—Karl Marx

Growing up, I saw no theater that mirrored my transgendered life, my patchwork gender. I wanted to express my life through my chosen work, but it just wasn't being done, so, like a chameleon, I lived my theatrical life day to day, rather than putting it up on the stage. I learned to live my life like I'm making a collage, and my theater follows that pattern. My queer theater consists of elements I gather along the way.

> Speaking, my accent still echoes this chameleon quality—
> you can hear in me traces of New Jersey, New York,
> Toronto, Alabama, California, Philadelphia, and London by
> way of Saskatoon.

First and Second Theaters

My experience in theater is grounded in naturalism and the Aristotelian model. I grew up with Eugene O'Neill, Tennessee Williams, Lillian Hellman and that gang—lots of reach-into-your-guts-and-pull-out-the-still-beating-heart; but I was looking to pull rabbits out of my hat. I found theatrical magic in Broadway musicals, people suddenly bursting into song at their most emotional moments.

In college, I waded through the identity politics of Albee and LeRoi Jones, without ever really discovering their identities. I stumbled over the magical unrealism of Brecht, Artaud, Jarry, and Beckett, but I was too stoned to incorporate their styles into my work at the time. Despite that, I was usually involved in the more conservative student theater organizations and productions—the Aristotelian model of conflict/resolution and moral integrity was the only theater I studied in depth, a theater designed to teach morality to a generally immoral theater-going audience. It wasn't until very recently that I had the luxury of really being able to study alternate forms of theater.

> In 1969, I broke rank and joined Judith Malina and Julian
> Beck for a few days in The Living Theater Company—my
> photograph is still somewhere in **Playboy** magazine,
> bending over, my backside to the camera, wearing only
> my jockey shorts. A close friend of mine, Gail Harris,

convinced me to leave the Living Theater and return to finish college.

My life drifted lazily between classes, rehearsals, performances, relationships and drugs. I got it that I could act—I would be tragic and audiences would cry, I would be comic and audiences would laugh. But none of that tragedy was mine. None of the humor came from inside me. I didn't know what was important to say or what was worth performing. As an actor and director, I felt I was someone who could interpret others' voices, but that I had no voice of my own.

"Kathy I'm lost," I said,
though I knew she was sleeping.
"I'm empty and aching and I don't know
why—
counting the cars on the New Jersey Turnpike.
They've all come to look for America."
            —Paul Simon and Art Garfunkel,
                    America, 1968

1985: I'd just begun living part-time as a woman. The Church of Scientology, IBM, and the tatters of my third and final marriage were behind me. I drove up from Philadelphia to New York to see Charles Ludlam perform *The Mystery of Irma Vep*. I was expecting a guy in drag. Instead, Ludlam transformed his gender on stage from male to something not exactly female—but transformed nonetheless. Ludlam incorporated elements of naturalism in his work, as well as elements of physical comedy. The result was fluid, highlighting the best of both naturalistic and magical elements.

Ludlam's multi-gendered life reverberated throughout his work: he performed from behind a fourth wall, regularly peeking out, and acknowledging the presence of the audience.

In 1986, just after my genital surgery, I directed a production of Jane

Chambers' *Last Summer at Bluefish Cove* for the Philadelphia-based feminist theater company, Order Before Midnight. This is when I found out that some art offends some people. Our production of *Bluefish Cove* was the Philadelphia premiere of the play, but *The Philadelphia Inquirer* and the other mainstream (non-lesbian/gay) papers refused to review us.

Additionally, some women from the local lesbian separatist community boycotted us on the grounds that I was involved with the production. It was the first time I experienced what was to become a recurring alliance against transgendered people: the conservative elements of both heterosexual and lesbian politics could find a common ground in decrying a transgender life and a transgender art.

Chambers' style was wonderfully corny, and steeped in the Aristotelian model: story line, characters who go through conflict, and a resolution. It was a portrait of lesbians, written by a lesbian, using what had previously been used to portray only a heterosexual model. The style of the piece is almost television sitcom, a style more accustomed to bashing gays than singing their praises. Chambers appropriated elements of an oppressor's art, putting them to use in the portrayal of a minority point of view. By doing that, she was able to communicate to folks who were accustomed only to a straight, naturalistic format. She didn't have to re-invent the wheel, she was free to use it in ways the wheel-makers never dreamt of. By seeing non-conventional people acting within a conventional model, the audience learns that lesbians are real people.

Traditional form permits an audience to experience non-traditional content in relative safety.

The next component of my queer theater came from a production of *Upwardly Mobile Home*, written and performed by Split Britches, a feminist theater company from New York. Like Ludlam, Split Britches members Lois Weaver, Peggy Shaw, and Deborah Margolin shifted the *form* of their theater, so that the form itself emulated a queer life. Instead of a linear story line, there were many stories woven together, each beginning and ending at different times; and instead of conflict and resolution, there was transformation.

[In our work,] we try to build in as many layers as we can, because reality isn't simple. Reality isn't just one story line. In that sense, it's possible for people to enter our work at different places, and our work becomes accessible to our audiences at different levels.

—Lois Weaver, in conversation with the author, 1989

The strength of the queer community in San Francisco in the late '80s showed up in the strength of its theater—both theater and community were out of the closet. Which came out *first* doesn't matter—it was a partnership between the community and its theater, one leading the other at different times in their mutual development. By the mid-'80s, many gay men and lesbians were not simply negotiating for assimilated positions in the culture, they were clamoring for attention, and their theater clamored along with them. Inspired by their bravery, I began to demand attention for my transgender issues. In the summer of 1988, I attended a theater conference, and performed there as part of a panel. I wanted feedback.

Kate Bornstein recreates three theater scenes out of her acting past—macho make-out artist Tolen's advice on getting birds, from Ann Jellicoe's 60s play, **The Knack**; *two bits from* **Happy End**; *a monologue from Jane Chambers'* **Last Summer at Bluefish Cove**. *Bornstein is transsexual and lesbian. When she performed in the Jellicoe play, she was still male, but says that, feeling alien to Tolen's type, s/he had* *to be coached to play him. Shades, leather jacket, attitude. The performance is very funny, what the audience knows bouncing off Tolen's words—"Women aren't individuals, they're **types**, no, not types, just **women**, they want to be **dominated**." Woman playing former male self playing male.*

*Bornstein did **Happy End** while saving money for the operation. A dual role. The director had invented an androgynous narrator/emcee à la **Cabaret** who also acted the female mob leader, in drag. Bornstein's San Diego performance is bittersweet, early Brecht, with an added canny mockery of drag's mockery. Woman playing former straight male self playing gay man playing straight woman. The Chambers came five months after the surgery; her re-creating is naturalistic, unlayered except by what we already know. I find it ordinary after so much sex-identity vertigo and role critique. But Bornstein says, deadpan, "I've come to see the gendered body as an accomplishment."*

—Erika Munk, *The Village Voice*, 1988

It was the first time in my life I felt I had something of my own worth saying—something that raised questions.

Watching her perform, I was unsettled by my awareness that Bornstein has no neutral body, that even her biology is not immutable but constructed. Is this the death of character? Where is the truth in this experience?

—Jill Dolan, *The Drama Review*, 1989

Hidden: A Gender grew out of that performance. Women at the conference kept coming up to me asking me when I was going to perform the full-length version of "this new piece," and they would ask me the title. Well, the big buzzword that year was **agenda**. Everyone was talking about this agenda, or that agenda. I made a joke that I had a hidden **agender**. John Emigh encouraged me to write the piece, but I'd never before considered writing about that part of my life.

Around this time, Holly Hughes was performing her one-woman show, *World Without End*. Hughes performed her life with an achingly beautiful blend of humor, strength, sarcasm, and vulnerability. Using pieces of her very personal life, she spoke on stage what had been forbidden in polite conversation. That was the key I needed to begin writing my own work. Hers was the artistic courage I was looking for. I'd been working diligently at blurring the lines between male and female, the cultural binary of gender. Watching Hughes perform, I descovered it's both possible and necessary to blur the lines of another culturally constructed binary, life and art. I wrote *Hidden: A Gender*, and it was co-produced by Theatre Rhinoceros and Outlaw Productions.

If it's been bottled up inside you for a long time, if it's been gnawing at every hour of your life, if it makes you cringe to think that people might find out, it would probably make a great piece of theater.

Work is love made visible.
    —Kahlil Gibran

A Cavalcade of Stars: Live (for now) on the Queer Stage!

Hidden: A Gender was selected to represent Theater Rhinoceros at the First International Lesbian and Gay Theater Conference and Festival, sponsored by the Alice B.

Theater in Seattle. "Selected" might be too kind a word. A play called **Lust and Pity** was actually selected, but in the true style of Mickey Rooney, Judy Garland and '40s musicals, the cast of **Lust and Pity** couldn't make it, and so, like Mickey and Judy, we were on.

The First International Lesbian and Gay Theater Conference and Festival took place within days of the announcement by John Frohnmeyer, then Chairman of the National Endowment of the Arts, that the Endowment would be rescinding grants to a number of artists who had been judged by their peers as deserving of that money.

We'd been told all our lives that we were bad and undeserving, and despite that, we did our art, brought our lives into the open—only to be told by some faceless power structure that our lives, our work, was indeed bad and indeed undeserving.

There's a real chance for a blacklist these days. A real chance. It's apparent in the lack of response from the Left to the Right's blatant appeal to homophobia. They want us dead.

*As to my NEA grant being rescinded, people call me and they say, "This will be the best thing for your career, Holly," and I say Fuck You! Fuck you! Be **me** for a day!*
—Holly Hughes

What's convenient for the government is that they keep getting this scapegoat called the queer voice. Hey—silence does equal death, and we are being silenced. And you know the scary part? The scary part is that the people voting on this haven't even seen the work—they're reading lies. The majority

of people are reading lies.
—Lori E. Seid, at a panel at The First
International Lesbian and Gay Theater
Conference and Festival, 1989

Censorship became the buzzword, and nearly, but not quite, the entire focus of the conference. We tried to figure out ways to get the work done—in spite of the efforts to silence us.

Holly is not exaggerating—they do want us dead. The what-is-to-be-done question looms large for me, and what I'm afraid of is that this period will signal self-censorship to young artists. We need to continue to blur the lines—find common ground with each other—continue to open possibilities for cultural exchange. And we need to develop a sort of underground railroad of performance spaces for lesbians and gays to do their work. Well—if they can't get grants, they can get work.
—Tim Miller, at a panel at The First
International Lesbian and Gay Theater
Conference and Festival, 1989

This year, it's the solo lesbian and gay artists. Next year, it will be the organizations called lesbian and gay. The following year, it will be the groups and institutions that systematically **hire** *lesbian and gay artists that have been refused grants. You get the picture—the line is creeping up.*
We need all of us to keep saying the words lesbian and gay. We have to educate people that we exist and that we are amazing! We have to come out and reach out with our

*work. We **have** to come out.*

  —Susan Finque, at a panel at The First
  International Lesbian and Gay Theater
  Conference and Festival, 1989

I'm a somewhat reluctant activist. My reluctance comes from the sad fact that even after the lesbian and gay revolution is over and won, there are going to be people dumping on me as a transsexual, or for being into S/M. I want to give my power to a movement that will speak *my* name as well.

At the conference, I found a theater with the potential to include anyone who will wear the name "queer"; and that includes me as both a transsexual and as an S/M dyke. We were united at that time against this seemingly monolithic oppressor, the U.S. government, which was coming down heavily on queer folks by trying to wipe out our artists.

> As I'm writing this, there's a new president in the White House, things are looking up for queers, and it was only as the final draft of this book was being prepared that the government agreed to settle and make restitution to the artists for wrongs done by the NEA under the Reagan and Bush administrations.

Part of the reason queer theater is inclusive is because it's had to be— we face a common oppression, and we need to unite against it.

How do we know how to seek out and learn about other gay people when they are so invisible, so ridiculed and diminished by everything that we see and hear?

 The effeminate man has been, and remains, the laughing stock of our movies, our most successful comedians. The butch woman is an object of particular scorn—but then, all women are.

 Homophobia and misogyny are not related.

THEY ARE THE SAME! The man who makes
an object of himself is beneath contempt.
And the woman who refuses to be one must
be stopped. The fact that we wish to be our-
selves and choose our same [gender] as
partners is the most threatening idea to
those who will never examine themselves.

— Craig Lucas, at a panel at The First
International Lesbian and Gay Theater
Conference and Festival, 1989

Sex and gender outlaws have needed allies. An empowering theater is a strong partner: a space in which people can work together for a common goal of freedom. But queer theater has been inclusive going a long way back. Lesbians, gay men, bisexuals, transgendered folks, S/Mers, all trace their roots to early cultures' shamanic rituals of transformation. These shamans were the healers, the mystics, the channelers of the truth of their time. They were the tricksters, the jokers and jesters and poets; they were the whores and the priestesses.

As whores and poets, they traded in love.

What's important is loving the audience. It's
not about what you feel as a performer when
you're up there—it's not about your per-
sonal catharsis. As an audience member, I
want you to make **me** *feel something.*
That's why I come to the theater. The artists
I have the most respect for, and I'm most
moved by, are those who give so much of
their hearts. To me, a good performance is,
in its essence, an act of love.

— David Harrison, in correspondence
with the author, 1993

As jesters and priestesses, our queer ancestors traded in the healing arts.

What we do is we choose stereotypes as
characters, but then we inhabit them as per-
formers. And we twist these stereotypes,
because that's what happens when you
inhabit what has hurt you. There's something
very healing about loving the people who have
hurt you the most, and then literally taking
them on. It's a way the world can help itself.
  —Deborah Margolin, in conversation
          with the author, 1989

Our ancestors played around with gender, as well as with sexuality. And their rituals were theater. Our ancestors performed their rituals, their theater, to heal themselves, and to heal their tribes. I *like* that heritage— it's one I don't mind trying to live up to.

> It's strange how that heritage has become buried. It's strange that while there are so many queer people in theater, the institution of mainstream theater is, like most of today's world, homophobic, and so the queer people in theater stay to themselves. They become isolated.

I was always fascinated with the relationship between the spiritual and the theatrical. Raised a conservative Jew, I nearly converted to Catholicism, so drawn was I to their ritual theater. But just as neither conservative Judaism nor conservative Catholicism speak to me or for me these days, a conservative theater also frustrates me. Theater that grows up in a community, with the aim of supporting that community, will become a theater that pacifies its audience. Its aim will be to pre- serve, and it will not provoke rebellion, but rather promote the commu- nity's status quo. In the same way that a fool and a shaman must, for their continued survival, stay free of attachment to any community, so must a theater stay free of any attachment to a community.

> Some of the most skillful theater I've seen is cranked out these days for the church of consumerism. This art is

commissioned in the name of advertising and public relations. Maybe several hundred years from now, we'll look
back on this art and really appreciate its beauty apart
from its politics, just as today we admire works of art
commissioned by the Catholic Church hundreds of years
ago. But remember that church work was commissioned
to keep people in the fold of Catholicism. Similarly,
today's advertising art is commissioned to keep people
nestled deep within the fold of materialism.

In choosing to break from the patron church of capitalism, the queer
artists at this conference found themselves seriously underfunded,
underpaid, and alone. A number of queer theater artists expressed the
feeling that the conference was "home." That they'd met their own kind.
That it was family.

*The problem is, we've been doing our work
in isolation from one another. A lot of us
became aware we can't do that any more.
We're not in competition with each other
like in straight theater—we do tend to work
together, and we gain so much more. The
topics we talk about may be different, but
we are united in style. The style, or structural device, seems to be a blending of
genres into one piece.*
—Noreen C. Barnes, at a panel at The
   First International Lesbian and Gay
Theater Conference and Festival, 1989

As outlaws—lesbians, gay men, transgendered, bisexual, or as S/M
players—we lampoon the images of the dominant (*i.e.*, heterosexual)
culture. We blend, fold, and mutilate popular forms and genres and
claim them for ourselves. The end result is oddly cohesive and coher-
ent. Camp, drag, and dyke noire drama are all examples of this melange
of barbed comedy.

*I learned about theater from a group of drag
queens in a theater company called Hot
Peaches, way back when. I learned a lifestyle
of sharing and healthy competition. Where
being good meant you had to wear higher
heels, sew more sequins onto your costume,
and dye your hair a funnier color than anyone else's. Succeeding meant stepping in
front of somebody else on stage so you could
be seen, and talking louder than somebody
else so you could be heard.*

*And I finally said to all these guys, "Hey,
there's no material here about women in
this group." And they looked at me and said,
"So, what's **your** problem? Write some."*

—Peggy Shaw, in conversation with the
author, 1989

Because we are in the process of lampooning the stereotypes of our
oppressors, we are aware of stereotypes evolving in our own subculture,
and we'll lampoon those as well. The queer theater artists I met were
unwilling to further any type of stereotypes in our community.

*From the scripts we keep getting, it seems
that Lesbian theater is still in the kitchen.
We have plays about lesbians eating, lesbians coming out to each other. We want to
get beyond that.*

—Faith McDevitt, at a panel at The First
International Lesbian and Gay Theater
Conference and Festival, 1989

If queer theater is nothing else, it *is* a good belly laugh—an irreverence
for what is the assumed normal heterosexual pattern of relating. Queer
theater steals heterosexual mating rituals and makes them gaudy, or
strips them bare, or turns them inside out. Our men seduce their men,

and this is embarrassing. Our women seduce their women, and live without their men, and this is unforgivable.

What Makes This Theater Different?

At a recent Theater Rhinoceros production of **Boys in the Band**, a man sat outside the theater selling rotten tomatoes for audience members to throw at the actors. Lesbian women picketed the San Francisco Lesbian and Gay Film Festival for screening **The Killing of Sister George**. Some folks look at **Tea and Sympathy** as homophobic and out of date. And I'm not sure that Jane Chambers would like it if she knew the hushed and awed tones with which her name is uttered in some circles.

Queer theater is in a continual state of flux, just like the queer sensibility from which it's born. We would do well to respect the queer theater pioneers, artists like Mart Crowley, Lillian Hellman, Jane Chambers, Tennessee Williams, Gertrude Stein and Oscar Wilde. We need to respect them, but not hold them up as the yardstick for ourselves or other queer artists.

Rather, we'd do better to measure our theater according to what we need and want our theater to accomplish—for ourselves, our audiences, and for all the people who will be touched by our audiences. In my particular brand of queer theater, I want to challenge people's concepts of gender and identity. I want the very act of my assuming another identity onstage to call into question the identity of each and every audience member. Accordingly, when I attend theater, I want my own rigid notions of identity to be shaken up. With this in mind, I've come up with my personal guidelines for a queer theater.

›› I look for a theater with artists who focus on self-discovery; too many actors and directors today look to be discovered.

›› I identify with and see the need for a theater with an outsider mentality, which tends to be considerate and inclusive of the excluded.

Most mainstream theater I see assumes a centralist position, tending toward elitism.

›› I look for theater that provokes, not theater that pacifies.

›› I don't like theater that assumes or promotes the idea that any identity is superior to any other, or that any images of the culture are sacred because they belong to those with a superior identity. I get excited by theater that struggles to occupy, re-define, and re-shape the heretofore sacrosanct images of our culture.

›› The realism we're accustomed to in most theater consists of a linear story line or, at best, a series of entwined linear story lines. For me, realism may be layered, intricately woven, and non-linear.

›› I look for theater that focuses on transformation, because I go along for the ride and am myself transformed.

›› The richest moments in theater are moments infused with love. It can be love gone sour, love gone awry, or unrequited love. It can be hidden love, obsessive love, or a love destined to destroy nations. Love that is spiritual, love that is carnal, love that is all in the mind. This love can be romantic love, brotherly love, sisterly love, or a combination of all of the above love. But of all these loves, the most powerful is unconditional love. Not surprisingly, unconditional love is the most difficult to portray onstage.

›› I'm especially tired of watching theater that limits itself to the portrayal of heterosexuality—and heterosexual romance only. I look for theater that portrays open sexuality and a wide range of eroticism.

›› The sexual power I have seen portrayed in theater has most often been represented in images of abuse, rape, and sexual violence against women and children. I'm looking to see sexual power portrayed as safe, sane, and consensually sadomasochistic.

›› Most theater admits to only two genders. I want to see theater that hasn't stopped counting.

›› I like humor and comedy. A lot. Even slapstick humor so long as it pokes fun at those in power. But a good deal of today's slapstick is still aimed at unempowered minorities. Camp is an alternative to this kind of slapstick—camp is zen-like in its irreverence for the established order, its non-violence, and its often dizzying use of paradox.

›› I live in the constructs of this culture day after day—I don't need a theater that simply portrays more of the same. I like to see theater which uncovers the rickety framework on which are draped the lies of the dominant culture.

›› Theater funded by the war chests of capitalism usually ends up a tool of capitalism, in the position of being yet another commodity. Theater funded by the community it supports can then be a tool by which an alternate community may be forged and/or strengthened. But any funding is dangerous if it ties the theater to the funding agent. At some point, queer theater must break ties with its funding sources and seek new sources of income which won't tie it down.

›› There's a debate that continues to rage about some nebulous thing called "quality of work" and about what's "professional theater" and what's art, and what's not, and what's obscenity and what's not. I'm tired of supporting theater that seeks to establish itself amongst the canonized classics of this petrified culture. I'm tired of supporting the canon of classics by which all theater is judged, and by which artistic measure is taken. Quality of work can only be measured in the moment, and by those in attendance at the work itself. Increased attendance at theater brings about higher standards of quality. Textbooks about quality, and critics' comments on quality, do not bring about higher standards, but only encourage a uniformity of standards. I'm looking for a theater that seeks no judgment outside of itself—a theater which constantly accomplishes its own aims, continually making itself obsolete. Eventually, this theater moves aside for the next wave of theater artists. There's no question as to whether or not it is art. Of course it is.

>> The final measure of a theater piece is this: Did it connect with the audience? Technical expertise is valuable in that it provides the artist with proven methods of connecting with the audience. If the subject of the piece is loving and true, it will connect with the audience— that's the heritage of the fool, the heritage of our shamanic ancestors.

Queer Theater as a Third Space

This type of theater has emerged variously, as theater of the oppressed, theater of the absurd, and revolutionary theater. It's the theater that has risen up in the face of oppression. It's not always been queer, and it won't remain fixed within the queer subculture. But it seems that lesbians, gays, transgendereds, bisexuals, and leather sexers now have a shot at making a major contribution to world theater, and we might as well run with that for as long as we can.

This type of theater could also be called Theater of the Third Space, and it would include members of any borderline community or non-community; it would include anyone who falls through the cracks of the cultural floorboards; it would include anyone who challenges a cultural binary; it would include anyone who is Other. We could call it Freak Theater, or Other Theater, but I'm for calling it Queer Theater, because we're the ones who have the courage and the sense of humor to be doing it these days. I *like* calling it Queer Theater, because it's nice to have something important with *our* name on it for a change.

Queer Theater is not lesbian and gay theater, just like not all lesbians, gays, and transsexuals are queer. Lesbian and gay theater was, at one time, cutting edge, more for its content than any style, but there's a complacency that lesbian and gay theater seems to be slipping into. The early '90s saw a number of lesbian and gay plays, playwrights, and performers achieve mainstream recognition; that's when the negotiating for assimilation began in earnest. Much of the community's theater followed suit.

Theater which had once signaled the charge out of the closet, began again to call up the kitchens and bedrooms of our lives. No longer was this community theater raising questions and implicating people, instead, it concentrated on "empowerment," and providing "positive role models." Queer Theater is shifting—continuing to thrive, but within the smaller venues, the low-budget spaces like Highways in Santa Monica; or P.S. 122 in New York; San Francisco's Josie's Cabaret and Juice Joint, or Red Dora's The Bearded Lady Cafe; Patrick Scully's cabaret space in Minneapolis; Real Art Ways in Hartford, Connecticut; The Drill Hall and the Institute of Contemporary Arts in London; and the It's Queer Up North Festival in Manchester. Through these venues, and through the more daring larger spaces like the Walker Art Center in Minneapolis, and through on-campus productions at colleges and universities around the world, Queer Theater is continuing to flourish and evolve.

Step by small step, queer artists are crossing over to reach broader and broader audiences, but many queer artists still hold down part-time jobs in addition to their full-time artistic careers. The economy has begun to dictate not only our venues, but also the size of our productions. Solo performers and small companies of actors, dancers, and comedians are touring the world—from Michael Kearns' series of brilliant solo performances focusing on AIDS to The Five Lesbian Brothers' darkly comic chronicles of the lesbian position in the culture. We're seeing each others' performances, and we're learning from one another what works. Our own patchwork individual identities have come together to form a brilliantly complex mosaic of theater for our day—a theater which will, hopefully sooner than later, seem passé and reactionary. It takes that kind of diversity of work and workers to maintain a Third Space.

It stands to reason that one day, some student will be poking around in some old library books. And she'll blow the dust off these books and there'll be works in there by Split Britches, or Doug Holsclaw, or Holly Hughes, or Leland Moss. And she'll read this stuff and maybe she'll yawn and say "yeah, so?" Or maybe there'll be a revival of **The AIDS Show**, or **Hidden: A Gender**. And maybe there will be someone sitting outside the theater selling rotten tomatoes in response to such reactionary, homophobic, or (god forgive the word) "transgenderphobic" work. And that just means that we as queer theater artists will have done our jobs very well indeed, and the artistic banner will have been passed on to the next and more enlightened generation of transformational artists in the spirit of Charles Ludlam—the spirit of the trickster, the shaman, the mystic performer, the outlaw.

And until that time, my feeling is that today we need, as queer artists, to strengthen our outsider sensibility, keep it fluid enough to be inclusive of other groups, inflammatory enough to challenge and wear down the dominant ideology, and full of enough grace and humor to welcome with a laugh the inevitable challenges to our own rigidity.

*Promotional photo for the first tour of **Hidden: A Gender**. (left to right) Justin Bond, Sydney Erskine, Kate Bornstein.*

hidden: a gender

"...the boys and girls in marketing have come up with the ultimate marketing strategy. We're not going to sell you any products tonight, no, we're going to sell you gender. And you want to buy it.

You want to buy gender because you want to relieve the nagging feeling that you're not quite a man, you're not quite a woman."

— Doc Grinder

*Doc Grinder (Kate) as "The Girlfriend," and Herman (Sydney Erskine)
in the first production of **Hidden: A Gender**.*

HIDDEN: A GENDER

a play in two acts

There are very few if any guidelines I can suggest or would require for performing this piece—"the vision thing" is ultimately the responsibility of the production company, and I'd love to be surprised by a new interpretation and new production elements.

Hidden: A Gender can be performed by any number of actors, in any number of gender configurations, and with any sort of staging. In this edition, I've included stage directions so that folks reading the play can get an idea of how we staged it originally. It's my hope that anyone producing the play in the future would cross out the stage directions before giving the script to the actors. It would probably be helpful to have a transgendered person with a good sense of humor involved with the production, perhaps as a consultant.

> Production rights for **Hidden: A Gender** are held by the publisher of this book; and they and I would love you to contact them about production information. I would certainly enjoy being in touch with anyone who's producing the piece, and I'm glad to be available to consult for any production of the play. You can write me in care of the publisher, or e-mail me at: OutlawGal@AOL.com.

Hidden: A Gender was first commissioned by Theatre Rhinoceros Literary Manager, Doug Holsclaw. It was first co-produced by Outlaw Productions and Theatre Rhinoceros, in San Francisco, November 1989, on the studio stage of Theatre Rhinoceros, under Artistic Director Ken Dixon.

The cast members were Justin Bond (Herculine et al), Sydney Erskine (Herman et al), and Kate Bornstein (Doc Grinder et al).

The production company was:

Director/Dramaturg...................................... Noreen C. Barnes
Stage Manager ....Sherry Anderson
Assistant Stage Manager ....Rick Garlinghouse
Technical Director, and
Stage Manager for the Tour .... Cayenne Woods
Sound Designer ....Lori Dovi
Choreographer... Drew Todd
Publicist/Graphic Designer..................................... Bobby Tyler
Production Photographer...Jill Posener

HIDDEN: A GENDER

a play in two acts

Act I, Scene 1

The staging is a unit set, and should suggest the studio and set of a television talk show program, like that of Geraldo, Sally Jesse, or Oprah. It should also include elements of the nineteenth century ancestor of today's talk shows—the traveling medicine shows.

There are three main playing areas. Down stage right is the space for the host/barker, Doc Grinder. A stool or podium may be used to suggest Doc's position of authority.

Up center is the space for Herculine/Abel. A period (nineteenth century French) chair, or bed, and a night stand would be ideal. Since she/he is an "exhibit," and since we are looking back in time at her/him, the lighting could be softer, or the space could be raised slightly, or set behind a scrim.

Down stage left is the space for Herman/Kate. In the original production, this was marked by a reclining leather chair, Herman's father's chair. Herman is also "on display," but since he is in current time, there is no need for different lighting.

DOC GRINDER

L.C. Doc Grinder is part twentieth century television talk show host, and part nineteenth century medicine side-show barker. It is never clear whether

Doc is a man or woman, and this ambiguity is never acknowledged by Doc him/herself. Doc speaks directly to the audience, and the actor playing Doc is encouraged to ad lib in response to any audience comments. The whole idea is to encourage the audience to play their part: the television talk show audience. In the original production of the play, the part of Doc Grinder was played by the playwright. Casting a transsexual actor in the role of Doc is not essential, but it does add a neat twist to the viewing of the piece. Doc's theme song begins—a pop rendition of the **Bahn Frei Polka**, *by Eduard Strauss. My idea of Doc is that he/she's a real charmer.*

If possible, Doc should enter through the audience, perhaps shaking hands, and then taking the stage with a bow that expects audience applause.

DOC GRINDER

Good evening, ladies and gentlemen. Thank you very much for coming this evening. Are you ready? I hope you're ready for suicide. I hope you're ready for perversion—for piety—for mutilation. I hope you're ready for scientific anomalies far too wretched to be described in mere words, and I am not talking about prime time television, ladies and gentlemen. No—I am talking about the subject of tonight's show, and that subject is—Gender Blur!

Hot one. I know. But you look liberal enough. You wouldn't be here tonight if you weren't, am I right? Of course I'm right. We are well-fed, well-educated people. We are creative. We want to write the script called America, and we want the starring roles. But—we do not want to be confused with the bit players. So—we do not cross clearly defined lines. And what's the most clearly defined line of all? Help me out here. That's right! It's the line marked Girl's Locker Room. Men Only. Ladies Room. Boy's Club—No Girls Allowed. Wimmin's Land—Wimmin Born Wimmin Only. We're looking for a few good men, and you've come a long way, baby. But baby—don't cross that line. Don't ever cross that line.

Ladies and gentlemen, you will tonight meet people who do cross that line—creatures from a world with which I hope you seldom have any contact. The World of Gender Blur! Gender Blur! We hate the very idea. We fear its practitioners. We scorn its victims. We are terrified to be touched by the taint of this offensive illness. Gender Blur. Why mention it in public, before men and women of good gender standing, such as yourselves?

Grinder's my name. L.C. Grinder. Doc Grinder. Proud of every moment of my life. Proud to have served humanity, in audience situations just like this and for over twenty-five years, by bringing to light news of every disease known to man, woman, and child, but never before have I mentioned Gender Blur—never before! Why now? Could be the moon. Could be the earth shaking under my feet. Could be it's time.

I'm going to brush aside the temptation to wax dramatic, ladies and gentlemen. Yes, I am. And I'm going to drop right down to the bottom line, and what's the bottom line—help me out here—that's right—it's money! My money. Your money. Legal tender.

Now, the boys and girls up in marketing all know that advertisements and commercials don't sell products. Advertisements and commercials sell what? Sex and gender! That's right! And sex and gender sell what? The products! Very good! Sex, because it's sex. And once you've had great sex, well, you're going to want more. And if you've never had great sex, you'll buy anything hoping to get some. But gender—that's another can of worms. That's a different kettle of fish. That's another pea in a different pod. Simply put, once you buy gender, you'll buy anything in order to keep it. You'll buy anything. So—the boys and girls up in marketing have come up with the ultimate marketing strategy. We're not going to sell you any products tonight, no, we're going to sell you gender. And you want to buy it.

You want to buy gender because you want to relieve the nagging feeling that you're not quite a man, you're not quite a woman.

(Going up to a woman in the audience.) You want to buy gender because you want to be secure in your gender identity, don't you, Sir? Excuse me, I am so sorry, ma'am, but that must happen to you a lot—you know what I'm talking about here. And you—you should not be smiling! Back to the show.

Ladies and gentlemen, you will tonight meet not one, but two pitiful persons of doubtful and dubious gender identity. Their stories will shock you, and will, I am sure, convince you of the need to define, enhance, and defend your own gender identities.

In this portion of the stage, and through the magic of Dramatic License, we shall peer into the past one hundred years ago. We shall travel in time and through space to France in the last half of the nineteenth century. There we will meet a beautiful, pious young schoolgirl named Herculine Barbin. Before your very eyes, the years shall pass as leaves falling from a tree, and you will observe her doubts, her fears, her worst dreams come true. If she were not so twisted, I could love her. A candle shall call forth her image.

Now, in this portion of the stage, a most distasteful character—quite alive, I'm afraid—who will entertain us with stories from his offensive and peculiar life. Mister Herman Amberstone. I? I'll be back from time to time. Just to check and see how you're doing. And to play the parts of other characters as needed. I shall always appear in this portion of the stage. But hush—I feel the presence of our young French beauty coming to life. Do not interrupt her, or she will disappear.

Doc leaves the stage through the audience, as the lights come up on Herculine.

Act I, Scene 2

TWELVE-YEAR-OLD HERCULINE

Herculine, in the original production, was played by male actor Justin Bond. Justin made no attempt at comic drag, but instead managed a carefully prepared cross-gendered performance. Herculine was written to be performed in a classic, fourth-wall style, including no interaction with the audience. She is on display, and doesn't know it. The scene could open with the sound of nuns singing in chapel. Herculine enters carrying a lit candle. The sound of the nuns singing fades under her opening lines.

…Holy Mary, Mother of God, pray for us sinners now and at the hour of our death. Amen. Oh, but Blessed Mother, I am so happy to be alive today. It's my twelfth birthday! Please don't let this be the hour of my death. Thank you. Amen. And now, I need to speak with you, Holy Mother. Don't think this bad, for I absolutely adore the day. I adore the school, and my classmates, and the Sisters. And I so look forward to becoming sensible, charming, literate, and happy the way the Sisters have promised. Sister Eleonore has told me that the road to being sensible, charming, literate and happy is marked by obedience. And I want to obey those who know better than me, Blessed Mother—it just seems at times that all—all know better than me. It gets rather difficult.

That's not why I need to talk with you. Last night, I slipped out of my dormitory again to visit Lea. I was so quiet no one knew I was leaving. The bedtime prayer had been said and Sister Eleonore was not in sight. I took up at random the first object at hand as I left my room—a little ivory crucifix of very pretty workmanship—you know the one, Holy Mother. I went without a sound to the room I knew to be Lea's. I held my breath and I bent toward her bed and I kissed her several times. I slipped around her neck—her white, soft, beautiful neck—the crucifix. And I said to her, "Here, my friend, accept this and wear it for me." Her beautiful blonde head came up toward me, and she thanked me with a kiss that was full of warmth. Oh Mother of God, I do hope you are still praying for me.

I had no sooner finished than I started—hastily—to go back the way I had come. Oh, Blessed Mother, I had not gone halfway when familiar footsteps made me tremble. My teacher was behind me and she had seen me. And so, Blessed Mother, I've just come from the office of the Mother Superior—you know how fond I am of her—where she told me she had almost struck me from the list of those to take First Communion this year. I began to weep. She motioned me toward her and she stroked my hair, forgiving me. Oh, Holy Mary—I left Mother Gabrielle with my heart penetrated by the sweetest joy and the deepest gratitude.

I believe that I read too much. I know I am to be innocent, but I have a passion for knowledge that I am told only boys may have. Nurse has told me that—"unremitting study might unsex young girls." But I continue to read. Is this disobedience, Mother Mary? Oh, please give me an answer.

As the lights fade on Herculine's part of the stage, and come up on Herman's, the voices of the nuns singing in chapel are heard again.

Hail Mary, full of grace, the Lord is with thee. Blessed art thou among women and blessed is the fruit of thy womb, Jesus. Holy Mary, Mother of God, pray for us sinners now, and at the hour of our death. Amen. Only, please don't let this be the hour of my death.

She exits, leaving on stage the burning candle.

Act I, Scene 3

HERMAN

*In the original production, Herman was played by female actor, Sydney
Erskine. As in the case of Herculine, no attempt at masquerading at another
gender was made—instead, a more ambiguous gender portrayal was stressed.
He's a man who's studied how to be male all his life, but for whom maleness
is foreign. Herman is written to speak directly to the audience, in a Brechtian
confrontational manner, but he does not have the freedom to interact with
the audience, like Doc. After all, Herman is an exhibit, a freak, a guest on
a talk show. Doc is in control.*

*Herman enters, somewhat self-conscious about appearing before the audi-
ence, but it soon becomes evident that he has done this before and is quite
adept at speaking to large numbers of people.*

This is my father's chair. One of the first rules I remember learning was that
no girls were allowed in this chair. Or if they did sit here, they had to pay a
quarter. When I was older, and I brought different girlfriends to my parents' house for a visit, I remember I would wait 'til my mother and father
had both gone upstairs, and then I'd sit in this chair with my girlfriend and
we'd make out, and maybe we'd even have sex on the warm, red leather.
And I'd always leave a quarter on the cushion before I'd go up to bed with
my girlfriend.

Sounds of children playing in a playground

I'm four and a half years old, my first day of nursery school. It's the first
social experience of my life outside of my family. These are the days when
the boys and girls have to play separately—so I start to go off with the other
little girls to play. And this teacher—I don't know her name, but I call her
Miss Tissue, because she always has a tissue in her sleeve—Miss Tissue says,
No No Dear, this is the line for the little girls. And I say, I know, I'm a little
girl. And you know the look that grownups can give you—the one that says
you are loathsome and sick and vile and about to be abandoned. She gives me
that look. And I know I'll have to pretend to be a little boy from then on.

Baruch atah adonai, elohanu, melech... I'm studying for my Bar Mitzvah! I just know the day I become thirteen, I'm going to become a man. I never really believed that, but I'm hoping the ceremony's going to do its job. On the way to Hebrew School, I pass this deli that has the *National Enquirer* in the window—you know, stuff like Parents Boil Baby and Eat It. This one week, there's this beautiful blond lady on the cover—and a huge headline that says "SHE WAS A HE." My heart stops. I try to read the article through the store window, but it begins on page three, and I know if anyone sees me staring at the paper the way I am, they'll know I'm a girl, and the jig'll be up. I pass this paper four schooldays in a row. I know that next week it'll be gone. Friday afternoon, I go in and buy the paper—I never had before, so I know the people in the store know I'm weird just like the beautiful blond lady on the cover. It's Christine Jorgensen. "Ex-GI, Now a Blonde Bombshell." "Look out, guys, that blonde cutie you're dating might have been one of Uncle Sam's finest men!" And then a quote from her—"I'm happy to have become a woman and I think more people who are as unhappy as I was before, should follow my example." I read that article over and over and over for a week. Then I burn it.

It wouldn't be for another thirty years that I'd read about Herculine Barbin and fall in love with her. But, back to the story.

It was in eighth grade English class when I learned more than I ever wanted to learn about gender. My teacher was Mr. Blunt. Good afternoon, Mr. Blunt.

Act I, Scene 4

MR. BLUNT

In the original production, Blunt was played by Doc Grinder in semi-clown get-up. He's a weary nerd of a high school English teacher. Because he's played by Doc, he addresses the audience directly, as though they are an unruly class of high school students, and he interacts with them accordingly.

Herman. Good afternoon, class. Today's lesson involves pronouns and gender. It is very important to use the correct pronoun to refer to the correct person—stop the snickering in the back row—all right, I'm only going to say this once, so you'd better take notes. I'm not going to repeat myself. Pronouns and gender. I has no gender. Neither does you. He and she definitely have a specific gender which is very helpful to all of—us—because we doesn't have a gender either. Does we? Back to he and she or rather to him and to her. He is masculine except when he is universal and means him and her and all of—us, who has no gender still. She is feminine, except of course when she is inanimate, like a ship or a salad, but six of one, half a dozen of the other, am I right? We still doesn't have a gender. You plural has no gender either. Unlike him and her, they has no gender whatsoever, which I will admit introduces some confusion, but we're almost finished so live with it. It has no gender at all, except of course when it refers to an infant about whose gender we are uncertain. Not unlike me. Or you. There will be a quiz next Tuesday.

A buzzer sounds, indicating the end of the class. Herman and Blunt exit.

Act I, Scene 5

17-YEAR-OLD HERCULINE

Enters running. In the original production, Herculine played this scene to an imaginary "Grandpappa."

Grandpappa! Grandpappa! Poppy, you've a letter from Paris, from your sister! Shall I read it to you? Yes, of course I shall. Sit, while I light another candle. I don't know why you so love dark corners. Here now—

"My Dearest Baptistin, I know it's been ages since I've written you, so my warmest greetings to you, dear Brother. And to you, sweet Herculine…"

She's writing to me too!

"…I know you are reading this to my crusty old brother. Your ghoulish grandfather adores sitting in the darkest corners of his house, so go, girl, and light another candle…"

Aunt Carmilla knows us each so well, Poppy—one would think she could read minds!

"…Very well then. Today, I was accused, in all sincerity, and by an otherwise sober gentleman, of being a vampire. Paris is going mad! I moved here twenty years ago because the Parisians celebrated artists and courtesans. Alas—now they call us vampires. Truly. Vampires are all the rage now…"

That's true—but the sisters will not permit us to speak of vampires.

"…From what I can piece together, loose women such as I are vampires because we…"

Loose women such as…?

"…loose women such as I are vampires because we desire the essence of men's fluids, and will stop at nothing to procure these precious fluids. Piffle. I've not been interested in a single man since Henri died, and that was over fifteen years ago. Babette and I have quite a comfortable arrangement, thank you very much. She is more of a woman than the frivolous coquettes who parade the Left Bank, and, I confess, more of a man than my sweet departed Henri…"

I—I know more than a few unusual girls like this in convent school.

"…Oh, poor Herculine, I am so sorry if I shock you, but according to my calculations, you are now seventeen years old…"

Seventeen years and five months, thank you.

"…and it's about time you heard about life in Paris…"

As if I didn't know about life in Paris!

"…Do come visit me, Herculine, and we can be vampires together! They say now that we women are creatures of darkness—that we belong only to the night, the moon, and the stars, Herculine. Brother dearest—you men, of course, have inherited the sun, the warmth, and the day. Ha!…"

Ha? Oh—"Ha!"

"…The irony is that I dare not go out in the streets at night for fear of personal injury. It's true there are no men out at night. Only beasts. If I am a vampire, then they are the werevolves…"

She must be speaking in metaphors. Yes. She is.

"…Speaking of blood—my anemia is much improved. I stop round the slaughterhouse with other blood-drinkers for my daily cup of ox blood, and that seems to help. Perhaps this medicine only further shows I am a vampire? Dear brother, I am enclosing for your pleasure Rachilde's latest novel, *Mister Venus*. It's a delightful story of a woman who keeps a man as her male mistress in an apartment…"

…male mistress?

"...watching him grow fat and slothful and passive in response to her possessive behavior..."

This is rubbish, Grandpappa. Still, I suppose it is readable.

"...Herculine, promise me you will become no man's mistress. I must run, my dears, the moon is rising, and I feel the urge to bite the neck of my sweet Babette..."

If she insists on doing these perversities with another woman, why does she insist on talking about them, and why to me? Why to me? She...

"...Your loving sister and aunt, Carmilla."

Vampires and artists, really! Grandpappa—Poppy, do you think someone, anyone, would go to Hell for doing what Aunt Carmilla is doing with Miss Babette?

Blackout. The candles remain burning, and Herculine exits.

Act I, Scene 6

HERMAN

Herman enters, picking up the book from Herculine's night stand, and thumbing through it, he walks over to his area stage left.

I'd read anything I could get my hands on. Anything that would tell me what I was. Who I was. What gender I was. Herculine learned about being a woman from the nuns, and from her aunt, the vampire. I watched television. I read *Life* magazine. I began to study acting. With each man's part I played, I learned more about how men were supposed to...act.

I was a good actor. In the late sixties, I played this motorcycle tough guy who could get all the women he wanted. I had no idea where to start and so my director had to coach me on how to move, how to talk, what to wear.

And I wore these dark glasses and I wore this leather jacket. I was in real bad boy drag. I even grew my sideburns yes I did. Bad boy. And my director he taught me how to walk—not like that, he'd say as I'd saunter across the stage. Not like that, you lead with your pelvis. Walk this way, he'd say, it's a pelvic thrust. And together we'd walk around the stage. And it was dark on that stage, with just a few rehearsal lights on, and I had these dark glasses and I couldn't see and walk this way he'd say and I'd let my penis do the walking, and I just went along for the ride, taking notes.

And I had lines like, "Women are not individuals, but types. No, not even types, just women. They want to surrender, but they don't want the responsibility of surrendering." And I thought to myself, yeah? Is that it? And I'd walk my walk, and I'd talk my talk and I learned how to get women. Yes I did. I learned to do whatever I had to do in order to get women. And I learned that once I got her, she'd do anything. I learned. And I walked this way, and the women lined up.

Enter The Girlfriend, played by Doc Grinder **en femme**. *The Girlfriend sits down on the stool in Doc's space.*

They just lined up outside my dressing room door. They wanted that stud. And I learned to be that stud. They wanted the leather jacket and they wanted the eyes they couldn't see and I wanted them so that's who I became. I wanted every one of those women. And one by one I fucked them and they fucked the character they'd just seen on stage. I fucked them over.

THE GIRLFRIEND
And despite all of that, he was still a sensitive kind of guy.

HERMAN
Trust me…

THE GIRLFRIEND
…he'd say to me…

HERMAN
…I understand you. Trust me…

THE GIRLFRIEND
…he'd say…

HERMAN
…I need you. Trust me…

THE GIRLFRIEND

…he said…

HERMAN

…I love you. I really love you.

THE GIRLFRIEND

How could you not fall for a guy like that?

HERMAN

And every night the lines outside the stage door got longer and every woman on that line convinced me I was a man. I learned. I was that stud. I learned. I had the Marlboro Man by the balls and I could fuck like the best of the boys. I learned. So I couldn't be a woman. Not if I loved women so much. I learned. How could I be a woman? How could I?

Act I, Scene 7

DOC GRINDER

Doc is still **en femme.** *Before this scene, Doc was a hardboiled male talk show host. Now, he's a more sympathetic* **female** *talk show host. Doc neither acknowledges nor makes any concession to this change in gender, which isn't exaggerated at all, but which is very different from his male persona.*

Yes, strange as it seems, he still feels like a woman. It's gender blur. We don't think about our gender day and night. Not like these poor victims. No, it doesn't even cross our mind. No. Not until someone calls you sir again. Not until someone says you're behaving too effeminately. Experts agree that we don't even think about gender in terms of ourselves. No, it's not until we see someone walking down the street and we can't tell if it's a man or a woman. Ever wonder why you can't stop staring until you decide one way or the other? It really bothers you, doesn't it!

We don't have to know someone's age. Their race may be somewhat indistinct, and we might be mildly curious. We may look at someone and think are they gay or straight, but we don't have to know. We can wonder. Yet we insist, and this is the curiosity, we insist that a person be one gender or the other and we remain unsettled until we assign one gender or the other. It's part of our conscience, isn't it?

And, as to conscience—we really should thank religion, whose chief task, it seems to be, is to see that we all have more or less the exact same conscience.

Herman comes up behind Doc, pushing his hips into Doc's backside.

My rod and my staff shall comfort me.

Herman and Doc tango off together.

Act I, Scene 8

HERCULINE

The tango music continues. Herculine enters, and stands facing the audience, as though she is examining herself in a mirror. We can see by the way she is touching herself and looking, that she is naked. She observes her breasts, muscles, cunt, long clitoris, beard. She is distraught, and enters a confessional. In the original production, this was done by Herculine walking to a small stool, kneeling on it, and speaking as if through a confessional window.

Forgive me Father for I have sinned. I fear I am becoming a vampire. My aunt is a vampire and she wrote me what it means to be one. My passion for God is at war with my passion for my studies. I am reading at every opportunity. And with every bit of knowledge I gain, I lose more and more of my innocence. I am falling away from all that is womanly. I am not interested in motherhood. I am not the least bit interested in arts and crafts. Two men have proposed marriage to me, and my response is revulsion. I...I am...My body—my body is changing.

Father, I do not yet desire blood, as does a true vampire, but I do desire a vampire's natural prey, namely other women. I have lustful thoughts and intentions for Therese, a student in my dormitory. We have kissed several times, and I take every opportunity I can to be near her, and to feel her so warm near me. I am frustrated with my own timidity, and at times I wish to play the part of a man with her. Oh, Father, I fear I am turning into a man. Listen to me. I know that carnal deeds are harmful and sinful. Why do I hunger so for Therese? How can I have a woman's passion for life and a man's thirst for knowledge? How can I have a woman's yearning for peace with my God, and a man's lust for women? What am I, Father?

My sins? Three nights ago, it was during the storm. I had stolen to the bedside of my Therese. I was stroking her hair, inhaling her scent, listening so carefully to her breath, her sighs. And then the terrible stroke of lightning and that awful clap of thunder. Father, I felt the hand of Our Lord pushing me away from her side. And I fought that. I clasped her to me, and though the wind howled and the nuns raised their voices in prayer, I held Therese and she held me. And with each peal of thunder we kissed so deeply and breathed our fear and exultation into each others mouths until, until we were both—exhausted.

If I am becoming a vampire, or if I cam becoming a man then I know I am falling away from God. Father—what am I?

Blackout. Herculine exits.

Act I Scene 9

HERMAN

Enters and sits in his chair.

I'd pray. I'd pray each night to wake up and be a woman. I'd pray in detail. Details like the taste and scent of every woman I'd slept with. Not their names. I was too stoned for their names. Details like going to sleep nights—sometimes alone, mostly not—but every night praying to God that I'd wake up and be a woman and every morning I'd wake up with a hand on my cock, sometimes my hand mostly someone else's—god they loved my cock and I never had the courage so say you do? you really do? well, hey then—take it, have it. Put it on the wall over your bed, just get it away from me. And it wasn't the cock so much as what the cock had me trapped in. I thought to myself, girl, you are one evil son of a bitch. You are one sick puppy. You had better crawl back into the hole you've been trying to dig yourself out of yes sir, girl.

And one day in Boston, Massachusetts, the lights went on. These big old 400 watt lamps went on in my brain and lit up corners of my mind I wished I swept up years before. I needed to find the answers to the world's problems, not mine! So I quit graduate school and got into my VW camper with my *I Ching* and my Tarot cards and my miso and my sprouts and I went off to Denver to climb a mountain and come down with the answer to the world's problems.

I needed hiking boots so I could climb the mountain. The store was closed, and next door there was this poster of an old monk in a cave, holding up a torch and looking into an open treasure chest. And the poster said, "Abandon Your Tedious Search—The Answers Have Been Found." And I thought—far out—what is this Church of Diabology anyway?

And I went in and these folks were eating pizza, and I thought— wow—enlightened and eating pizza! I read their books and they were on to me. Whole sections about perverts like me and how sick we were. Homoseckshuls, lesbins, rapists, psychiatrists, and politicians. And I thought—far out—if they can see how sick and twisted I am, then this is the group for me! Six years later, I'm their leading spokesman in Europe and the Eastern United States. I'd give these lectures. I'd sell immortality.

And they'd spend $250 an hour to get it. I'd sell this stuff thinking this is my spiritual penance, man, this is what I need to do so next lifetime I can be born a woman.

Hey—everyone wants immortality. It's a surefire sale. You want it, don't you? Oh, I don't mean in the same body you'd have the ability to choose your own parents next time around. Neat, huh? You can get started for only $25,000. And they wrote the checks—they just kept writing those checks. I gave 'em a show.

One day, I'm in the Diabology sales office in New York and this woman walks into my office and says she needs to see me. I ask her to sit down and she does and she's crying. Only she's going boo-hoo-hoo, just like that. Boo-hoo-hoo, boo-hoo, boo-hoo-hoo. Nobody really cries like that. And some of the other sales reps who knew her were standing in the doorway behind her and they were laughing real quiet so she couldn't hear. They were just bustin' a gut shakin' like jelly turnin' all red and she's going boo-hoo, boo-hoo-hoo. And it turns out she's a transsexual and she's had this operation to make her a woman and now that she's gotten into Diabology they've convinced her she's done the wrong thing and she wants to know if she pays enough money to me can she grow another cock and the guys in the doorway they just keep on laughing and I have to tell her I don't know if you can grow another cock. I don't know what I can do for you. I just don't know.

DOC GRINDER

Enters through the audience, taking the stage on his stool. He has both male and female elements.

I thought we cut that bit.

HERMAN

I, uh... left the Church of Diabology some years later when I found out that all the money I'd been making was going into the Swiss bank accounts of the Founder. And I was free to explore my—my gender blur. I started asking questions.

Act I, Scene 10

DOC GRINDER

Questions. Queries, conundrums, bones of contention. Questions. Quests. Did you ever go on a quest to discover your gender identity? You never had to sort that out, did you? Of course not. None of us do. Some of you should.

But, let us return in time. Our beautiful nineteenth century heroine has graduated and has obtained a teaching position in a private school for girls. Two years have passed. Herculine is once again carrying on—having an affair with another woman. This time it's Sara—the daughter of the headmistress. That is, until the night the pains began for Herculine, and a doctor had to be called in. It seems the good doctor found the source of Herculine's pains to be a pair of healthy testicles descending into her labia. Her otherwise perfectly formed vagina opened into no uterus. It was a dead end. Her clitoris was found to be an intriguing two inches long. Now—how did I know *you'd* like that part?

Bear witness now to what the doctor found. And the questions. Queries, conundrums, bones of contention. Questions.

Blackout. Doc and Herman exit in the darkness.

Act I, Scene 11

HERCULINE

A single pin spot illuminates only her face.

Why is he asking me all these questions! Oh-h-h-h-h-h what is causing me this pain? When did I last have my menstrual flux? Ha! I never have, and that's—o-w-w-w-w-w-w please may I have some more laudanum?

No man has seen me like he is seeing me now. I want his hands to stop touching ow-w-w-w-w-w! I wish Sara were here to hold my hand no I don't. No I don't. When does the laudanum begin to ease the pain, doctor? What does he mean by descending? Sara he won't stop—is it because I have loved you? I love you.

Testicles? Have I ever...with how many men? None! What is he speaking about—draining their semen their fluids in the night. What? I grow somewhat lightheaded. The laudanum of course of course of course I am a vampire. No—only women. Suck? Yes, of course. Ow-w-w-w-w-w!

Doctor, I have had no men in my life but the priests, my grandfather, and now yourself. I've—what's in that jar? One? One what? Two? What are those... GET THOSE LEECHES AWAY FROM ME! PLEASE! PLEASE! Don't! Please don't. Not up inside me! Oh no, no, no, no, no. My head is too cloudy. Three? Four! Four leeches up inside me am I loosing my mind? He has counted them aloud saying he wishes not to lose any. Leeching a vampire! Hail Mary full of grace the Lord is with thee blessed are thou among women and blessed is the fruit of thy womb oh Jesus I feel them moving inside me Holy Mary mother of God pray for us vampires now and at the hour of our death amen. Please, please let this be that hour!

Has what gotten longer? That? Sara calls that my man part yes you do my love. Yes. Yes it has since my arrival at the school. I've become a what?

Oh, no—no no no no no I am a woman. I am sensible I am charming I am literate I am happy I am what men are not. Men are busy—I am to be idle. Men are rough—I am to be gentle. Men are strong—I am to be frail. Men are rational—I am…I am rational. God help me I must be a man. What? Yes, more laudanum, of course. I have no uterus? What in heaven's name is a uterus? Oh.

Sara, he is saying I am a man. He is saying I am a man and I must obey him for I am nothing if I am not obedient why is my head spinning? Sara—two women cannot be lovers. It is obscene.

Four leeches are growing fat on the last traces of my womanhood and shortly I will be nothing but a man. I am a man. I have questions, Doctor. I do not question you. I have questions. I am a man. A man can question things, can he not?

Blackout.

Act I, Scene 12

DON'S VOICE

In the original production, this pre-recorded talk played in the blackness, and was performed by the same actor who plays Herculine.

Questions? Did somebody say questions? That can mean only one thing!

Drumroll.

Ladies and gentlemen, joining us tonight is our current champion. Over thirty years of successfully answering questions and tonight is the final night—the night for the grand prize—ladies and gentlemen, welcome our returning champ, Herman Amberstone, to the grand finale round of *What's My Gender!*

Canned applause, music. The lights come up to reveal a very puzzled

and nervous Herman seated on a stool center stage. The voice-over
continues.

What's My Gender—the fun question and answer game brought to you by
Doc Grinder's famous elixir, Gender Defender, in the pink and blue bottles.
And now for our Master, or is it Mistress, of Ceremonies—L.C. Doc
Grinder!

DOC GRINDER

Doc enters as the male game show host. The audience becomes a game
show audience.

Thank you, Don, thank you, and hi there, folks! Well, Herman, you're a
champ at this, but I'm going to review the rules for our studio audience.
We're going to be asking Herman some very intimate questions—anything
and everything about his, or is it her, gender identity. There are no right
answers, but our champ has to answer these questions to his, or is it her,
own satisfaction. Are you ready, Herman?

HERMAN

Yes, L.C., I am.

DOC GRINDER

All right! Then, let's play round one of... *What's My Gender!*
    Your first question—Herman, you may think you're a woman—aren't
you really just a gay man who's so afraid of being gay that the only way to
have sex with men is to be a woman?

Canned audience reaction—Ooooooooo.

HERMAN

No—no, L.C., I've thought about that one a lot—I don't want sex with men.
Tried it a few times to make sure...

DOC GRINDER

I'll bet he did !

HERMAN

…and I'm not cut out for that. So—I'm not a gay man.

Canned audience—aw-w-w-w-w-w.

DOC GRINDER

Hey—he's not a gay man! But that's just the first of our questions. The next question is…oh, this is a killer…Herman, can't you just dress up like a woman, occasionally, like a hobby?

Canned audience reaction—whoa-oa-oa.

HERMAN

It's not the clothes, L.C.—I feel I'm a woman no matter what I'm wearing.

Canned audience reaction—mmmmmmmmmmmmmm.

DOC GRINDER

Works for me. Tell you what, folks—let's take a short commercial break while we try to figure out his answer to that last question, and then we'll return to play… *What's My Gender!*

DON'S VOICE

What's My Gender is brought to you by Doc Grinder's Gender Defender, the miracle elixir that keeps you straight. In the pink bottles for girls, and the blue bottles for men. And now—back to our show!

DOC GRINDER

Here we are ladies and gentlemen—after over thirty years of successfully answering questions, and tonight's the final night! Are you ready, Herman?

HERMAN

As ready as I'll ever be, L.C.

DOC GRINDER

All right, big fellah, good luck to you. And the next question is—do you
have any idea of the privileges you'll be giving up that belong only to
heterosexual white men, and the limitations you'll face as a woman?

Canned audience—ooooooo!

HERMAN

Yes.

DOC GRINDER

That's it? That's your answer. Why, you... *(looks offstage)* Well, hey—Hey!
Bold move! A totally unjustified answer! And the judges are going to buy it.

Canned audience applause.

Don't get carried away!

Canned audience stops.

Now—the final question before we ask him *What's His Gender - (drumroll)*
Herman, how can you be a woman if you love women sexually and romantically?

Canned audience—assorted gasps.

HERMAN

My gender identity has nothing to do with my sexual preference. Gender
identity for me answers the question of who I am. Sexual preference answers
the question who do I want to be romantically or sexually involved with.
My being a woman does not mean I must love men. These are two separate issues.

DOC GRINDER

Two separate issues??!? What are you trying to...

Canned wild audience applause. Doc looks offstage to "the judges."

Of course they are. Two separate issues. I knew that one myself. We're going to return to ask him what's his gender, but first—Don, why don't you tell our studio audience what our champion will win... *if* he has the courage to go through with this.

DAWN'S VOICE

Don has become Dawn.

All right, L.C.—Herman has a lot to look forward to! If he or she wins and names his or her gender, then he or she wins one dozen bottles of ice blue Secret deodorant—strong enough for a man, but gentle enough for a woman. And two dozen pairs of Jockey shorts. Or Jockey for Her as the case may be. And three dozen pairs of Hanes support socks, or support panty-hose—either way, gentlemen prefer Hanes! And last, but not least, Herman will win a lifetime supply of Doc Grinder's Gender Defender, the miracle elixir that keeps you straight. Gender Defender—one bottle and your fears disappear! Two bottles and your family breathes a sigh of relief. Three bottles and you can vote Republican. Back to you, L.C.

DOC GRINDER

Thank you, Dawn—thank you very much. And now—it's time for the final question. The killer conundrum, the bone of contention. Herman Amberstone—for all those great products, and for a year's supply of Doc Grinder's Gender Defender, my miracle elixir that keeps you straight, in the pink bottles for the girls, and the blue bottles for the men—Herman, What's Your Gender?

From the audience come canned shouts of "Man, go for man!" or "Woman, be a woman!"

HERMAN

I'm a woman.

Doc laughs, snaps his fingers, signalling triumphant music, confetti, wild applause, cheers. Blackout.

Act II, Scene 1

The lights come up on the stage, catching by surprise the First Actor, played by "Herman," and the Second Actor, played by "Herculine." They are carrying a bucket, dustpan, and broom, sweeping up something from everywhere. Doc enters, unaware of the presence of the other two, and begins to speak.

DOC GRINDER

Given the luxury of self-examination…

FIRST ACTOR

DON'T MOVE TO YOUR LEFT!!!

DOC GRINDER

WHAT!!?!!

FIRST ACTOR

Sorry, you almost stepped in some.

DOC GRINDER

Thank you, I…almost stepped in *what?*

FIRST ACTOR

Gender—it's all over the place. Careful!

DOC GRINDER

Oh, well, I see, I…Wait a minute! Are you telling me you're sweeping up…gender!!

FIRST ACTOR

Yep, bucket's almost full. We lose a lot during the first act.

SECOND ACTOR

Tons. Just tons.

DOC GRINDER

And so there's gender all over the stage? *(sitting)* I don't see any!

SECOND ACTOR

Well, I'm not the least bit surprised—you're sitting in some.

DOC GRINDER

The gender on Doc's stool pokes and prods at Doc, who is trying valiantly to remain seated. One final shove from the gender, though, and he's tossed off onto the stage. The Second Actor cleans off a final bit of gender from the stool with a flourish.

Listen you—I've got one more monologue, and then you're on. Hadn't you better get ready!

SECOND ACTOR

To First Actor, ignoring Doc.

We have enough?

FIRST ACTOR

I think so—go ahead—I'll bring this back to the dressing room.

SECOND ACTOR

Bye, girls!

DOC GRINDER

(To Second Actor) You! Put that down, and get over here! Do you mean to tell me you do this every night?

FIRST ACTOR

Yeah, we usually do it during intermission, but tonight's a better audience, so there's a whole lot more—they lose some, we lose some—it adds up.

DOC GRINDER

Well, that makes sense, I…GET BACK OVER HERE! You mean everyone's gender is mixed up in there?

FIRST ACTOR

Yeah, so?

DOC GRINDER

There's male and female mixed up in here?

FIRST ACTOR

Oh! You think male and female is gender!

*Music under: honky-tonk version of **The Stars and Stripes Forever**.*

Nah, that's not gender. Gender is the feeling that you need to be one or the other. Gender is the need to belong—it doesn't matter to what. Gender is the need to fit in, be part of something. All the rest is marketing. Sales. Public Relations.

DOC GRINDER

Well, sure, then…GIVE ME THAT!

Doc pulls the bucket from First Actor, falling and spilling its contents onto an audience member in the first row. The gender is loose in the studio! He nervously approaches the audience member.

Do you feel any different? No? No! Of course not! Ha! Now *(To First Actor)*—don't you have some acting to do!!?!

FIRST ACTOR

Is this acting? Is this dialogue?

STAGE MANAGER'S VOICE

Hey, you guys—five minutes to the Marx Brothers bit.

FIRST ACTOR

Gotta run. You're so cute when you're angry.

First Actor exits.

DOC GRINDER

Yes, well. Ladies and gentlemen—forgive the interruption—this evening's entertainment is being brought to you by Doc Grinder's Gender Defender. The medicine so strong you don't even need to take it in order for it to work. One look at the bottle and you know what you are. In the pink bottle for the girls, and the blue bottle for the men.

But, my Gender Defender is only the latest in a long line of medical accomplishments in the field of Gender. Let us return to our two misfits, and see how their doctors cared for them.

Oh—you do know what "care" is, don't you? Care is a curious and efficient blend of love and hate—with none of the messiness of commitment and responsibility. As in under your doctor's *care*. As in I care about *you*. Deeply.

Act II, Scene 2

HERCULINE

Herculine enters, dressed awkwardly as a man, and speaks to an imaginary sleeping Sara.

Sara? Sara are you awake? Of course you're not. The doctor said those powders would cause you to sleep 'til noon tomorrow. It was the only way I could leave you, dearest. I know you don't want me as a man, and I must leave for Paris to begin my life as one. I must obey the doctor.

Oh, sweet love, I hope you will one day come to see, as I have seen, why I must do this. According to Dr. Tardieu, I am a man chiefly because I cannot bear children. The mysterious uterus is present nowhere in my body.

According to the Doctor, it was all the reading I did as a child that caused my uterus to vanish and my, um, man part to begin to grow. The good doctor agreed with Father Michael that too much knowledge is incompatible with the innocence which is women's nature. It's why I've loved women so intensely, and we both know how unnatural it is for two women to love one another as we have done. The doctor went on to say that while he heard I was an excellent teacher, that was simply further proof that my nervous system had indeed become male. He's really quite taken with my state of affairs—he says I am evolving from a lower life form to a higher one. That I shall soon be able to enjoy power, knowledge, and more women than I could ever imagine. Once my man-part grows in. He said I must practice my manhood rigorously, for androgynous character is often accompanied by imbecility, and he caught me just in time before my mind began to deteriorate. He said I've lived my life as a pencil sketch, and to prepare for a life as rich and as full as an oil painting.

You know I've never been quite happy with my lot, Sara. Perhaps I shall find happiness as a man. I am terrified. I know nothing of men, and I've been discontented with my life as a woman. I confess to a thrill at fulfilling a vast desire for the unknown. Sara, I am too full of excitement and too full of myself to regret the very dear ties I am breaking now of my own free will.

Sara—the doctor has laid such temptations at my door! He said that women, and other lower forms of humans, like the blackamoors and the orientals—that these lower forms of life are valued for, oh what did he say, they are valued for loyalty, intimacy, hard physical work, obedience, devotion, and their ability to serve and nurture men. Us. Me.

Can you see this is my escape? Can you see this is my freedom? Sara, I was never meant to be some man's wife or indeed the serving maid of anyone. Before this door to manhood opened, I had no path but the path of virtual slavery—or persecution as some vampire—for that is woman's lot. I only wish I had the courage to say this to you while you were awake. I was never brave. I'm sure that will come with time, and perhaps I shall visit you and...no. That will never be. I could never face you again. That part of me shall always remain coward.

Sara—we yielded to each other's love. What will it be like to fulfil my destiny as a man by conquering women? Dominating their desires? For all this has the doctor promised me. Good-bye my sweetest love. Forgive me one day. Good-bye.

Herculine exits.

Act II, Scene 3

HERMAN

Herman enters, dressed androgynously, and addresses the audience.

I'm transsexual, I said to my wife.
I'm not a lesbian, she said, goodbye.
I'm transsexual, I said to my friends.
We don't know you, they said, goodbye.
I'm transsexual, I said to my mother.
You're my child, she said, but for now goodbye.
I'm transsexual, I said to my boss.
Can you still sell, he said, get back to work.
I'll need time to go to the hospital, I said to him.
Goodbye, he said.
I'm definitely transsexual, I said to my first shrink.
I wonder, he said, how our therapeutic relationship would change,
he said, if he were to leave his home and his wife and his two children, he said, and
we were to shack up together, he said.
Goodbye, I said.
I'm transsexual, I said to the surgeon's nurse on the phone, and I'd like an appointment.
Two o'clock next Friday, she said, goodbye.

Herman exits.

Act II, Scene 4

This scene is done in the style and character of a Marx Brothers skit. Doc is

Dr. Razor, the Groucho figure. The actor playing Herculine plays both Nurse
Dimple, a Marx Brothers dumb blonde, and Dr. Weener, a Harpo charac-
ter. Herman plays the straight man.

NURSE DIMPLE

Two o'clock next Friday, goodbye. Razor and Weener, general surgeons, hello. No, Dr. Razor and Dr. Weener aren't in right now. They're in surgery. I expect them any moment. I'll be sure to tell them. Goodbye. Oh, good morning, Dr. Razor!

DR. RAZOR

Doc Grinder enters as Dr. Razor, wearing a white lab coat. Instead of a
cigar, he twirls a vibrator in his hand.

Never mind that, Nurse Dimple, get the hospital on the phone! Get the Surgeon General on the phone! I just finished a sex change operation, changing a man to a woman, and I made a terrible mistake!

NURSE DIMPLE

Oooooooo, doctor, whatever happened?

DR. RAZOR

I forgot to remove half the patient's brain!

Nurse Dimple laughs hysterically.

You know, I can never tell if she's laughing or if she's choking. Of course, that's the way it is with *all* my women.

NURSE DIMPLE

Doctor Razor! You have a message to call Frank's Fresh Fish and Bait.

DR. RAZOR

Frank's Fresh Fish and Bait? What do they want, nurse?

NURSE DIMPLE

They want their money, doctor.

DR. RAZOR

And exactly how much do we owe them, nurse?

NURSE DIMPLE

You owe them nine thousand dollars, doctor.

DR. RAZOR

Egad! That's the most expensive and delicate part of the whole sex change procedure!

NURSE DIMPLE

What's that, doctor?

DR. RAZOR

Sewing in the day-old fish!

He pulls a dead fish from his pocket, tossing it aside. Nurse Dimple chokes.

She's definitely choking now!

NURSE DIMPLE

Dr. Razor, they're not the only creditors calling! Bill collectors have been calling all morning! They say they're tired of phoning and something will have to be done!

DR. RAZOR

OK, we'll do something, nurse—marry me, and we'll move to the next state!

NURSE DIMPLE

Ooooooo, doctor!

DR. RAZOR

But seriously, nurse, we need a new patient with lots of money.

NURSE DIMPLE

Well, you have a Herman Amberstone coming in at two today—that's any minute from now, Doctor.

DR. RAZOR

Amberstone, Amberstone—hey, sounds Jewish to me!

HERMAN

Hello, you must be Dr. Razor.

They do a handshake bit, ending up with Dr. Razor slapping the vibrator into Herman's outstretched hand. The vibrator goes off, falling to the floor, buzzing away. Doc retrieves it from the floor, turning it off.

HERMAN

A good friend of mine told me you're an excellent sex-change surgeon.

NURSE DIMPLE

Ooooh, Honey—you just *think* that's a good friend of yours.

DR. RAZOR

Nurse Dimple, I'll handle the punch lines around here. Unless of course, you'd like a punch yourself!

Nurse Dimple exits, Dr. Razor follows her out, admiring her swaying der-riere, but at the last minute turns back to Herman.

Now, young fellow, what can I do for you?

HERMAN

Well, I'm here about a sex change.

DR. RAZOR

Sex Change! Why didn't you say so? I know what a sex change is! What is it? Sex of one—half a bosom of the other.

Herman attempts to leave.

Hold on there youngster, I'll call in my associate—Dr. Weener! Oh—DOC-TOR WEE-E-E-ENER!

NURSE DIMPLE *(Off-Stage)*

Doctor Weener! You masher!

Sound of slap, Dr. Weener enters with a rolling prat fall—replete with Harpo wig, white lab coat, and horn.

DR. WEENER

(honk)

DR. RAZOR

Well, hello, Dr. Weener!

DR. WEENER

(honk)

DR. RAZOR

You don't say!

DR. WEENER

(honk, honk)

DR. RAZOR

You don't say!

DR. WEENER

(honk, honk, honk)

DR. RAZOR

You don't say!

HERMAN

What did he mean?

DR. RAZOR

I don't know, he didn't say! Probably something very technical and very medical about the sex-change procedure we plan to use.

DR. WEENER

Running in circles around Herman, "examining" him lasciviously, while Herman is trying to fend him off with a chair.

(honk)

HERMAN

And what procedure do you plan to use?

DR. RAZOR

Leaning his head on Herman's shoulders, rolling his eyes.

For what, doll-face?

HERMAN

To make a new vagina!

DR. WEENER

(honk)

Dr. Weener demonstrates the procedure by pulling a banana from his lab coat, slowly peeling it, then breaking off a large hunk of banana and hurling it offstage. He turns to Herman, triumphantly.

(honk)

                          HERMAN
That does it. I'm outta here.

He attempts to leave, but is stopped by both doctors.

                          DR. RAZOR
Hold on there, young fellow. I'll have you know that we—Dr. Razor and
Dr. Weener—are the tops in our field. Why, we have diplomas from every-
where!

Both doctors open their lab coats, revealing many important diplomas.

And you won't find a better pair of surgeons in all of Philadelphia!

                          HERMAN
Oh, all right. You're the boss.

                          DR. RAZOR
I'm the boss? Well, that's more like it! In that case, get back to work. And
you can forget about your promotion.

                          HERMAN
I'm not getting a promotion?

                          DR. RAZOR
I should say not! You're becoming a woman, and that's a de-motion if I ever
heard of one ! So tell me, is your boyfriend going to help you out with the
money for the surgery?

                          HERMAN
I don't have a boyfriend.

                          DR. RAZOR
No boyfriend! Fiancé, then?

HERMAN

I don't have a fiancé.

DR. RAZOR

No fiancé! But you are seeing a man, aren't you?

HERMAN

No.

DR. RAZOR

But you are planning on marrying a man, adopting two-point-three children, a dog, a third of a cat, and a white picket fence?

HERMAN

Sometimes I think about a white picket fence. And I have two cats.

DR. RAZOR

Two cats! Are you telling me you're planning to become a...lesbian!!?!

The doctors are titillated beyond words, and bump each other in a bizarre
mockery of lesbian love-making.

HERMAN

Well, yeah, I guess so.

DR. RAZOR

Swell! That's been my favorite fantasy for years!

DR. WEENER

(honk)

HERMAN

Well, YOU'RE NOT MINE!

He tosses the doctors aside.

DR. WEENER

(honk)

Dr. Weener exits in a huff.

DR. RAZOR

I couldn't agree more, Dr. Weener. Why you—you're nothing more than a wolf in cheap women's clothing! I have my limits, my morals, and my ideals! You're obviously not a real woman. Still, you're awfully cute—can you get the money together?

HERMAN

How much?

DR. RAZOR

Let's see, the bait shop needs—I mean, I'll need nine thousand dollars, and I'll need it stat—whatever that means.

HERMAN

I don't have that much now.

DR. RAZOR

Then go, and never darken my office door again. You want an orifice? Don't come to my office *(pronounced to rhyme with "orifice")*! Not until you get the money!

I mean, not until you're more of a woman! Good day, sir!

HERMAN

I'm a transsexual lesbian, I said.
Goodbye, they all said.
That's just too much to handle, they all said.
One or the other, maybe, they all said.
But both, they all said, goodbye.
Goodbye.
Goodbye.

ACT II, Scene 5

DOC GRINDER

Sound under: percussion music. Doc is now very femme, and does the following as a macabre send-up of Laurie Anderson. Or maybe it's Rod Serling. One of those cultural icons.

Good-bye.
Hello.
It's now.
It's what you've been waiting for.
The woman destroys herself
to envision man.
The man destroys himself
to envision woman.
No simple masquerade, this.
To truly become the other gender,
the first gender must be
destroyed.

HERCULINE

My name will be Abel.
Child of peace, victim of aggression.
Beloved of God, slain by his brother.
Mourned through the ages.

DOC GRINDER

Sweet, and the boy?

HERMAN

My name will be Katherine. It was the name of a girl I wanted to be all through grade school.

DOC GRINDER

How childish.

HERMAN

It's my child within.

DOC GRINDER

Very well, children,
then walk in the sun
and let the flame of the public eye
burn away the remnants of
the man
the woman
you have been all your life.

*Doc stalks off stage. Rhythmic bells begin to play. Herculine and Herman
are losing their gender identities, each becoming more androgynous in the
following dance. The lines are said in an overlapping fashion, rhythmically
in time with the music, and repeated at the discretion of the actors and
choreographer.*

HERCULINE/ABEL

They're looking at me.
Their eyes are burning me.

HERMAN/KATE

They're looking at me.
Their eyes are burning me.

HERCULINE/ABEL

Is it my body?

HERMAN/KATE

Is it my hair?

HERCULINE/ABEL

Is it my voice?

HERMAN/KATE

Is it my skin?

HERCULINE/ABEL

Is it my movement?

HERMAN/KATE

Is it my movement?

HERCULINE/ABEL

Is it my emotion?

HERMAN/KATE

Is it my ambition?

HERCULINE/ABEL

They are...

HERMAN/KATE

...looking at me. Their eyes...

HERCULINE/ABEL

...are burning me.

HERMAN/KATE

I'm to be a woman, I said to the man
I once had been, goodbye he said.
Oh god, I'm disappearing.

HERCULINE/ABEL

It is as though I come apart from
myself. No longer woman, not yet
a man. Standing outside.
Bidding myself adieu.

*They have no more identity. Herman becomes One. Herculine becomes
Another. They hear each other for the first time, and search for one another.*

ONE

Goodbye?

ANOTHER

Goodbye?

ONE

Goodbye?

ANOTHER

Goodbye?

They find one another on stage, and embrace silently as part of the dance.
The music stops.

DOC GRINDER

Doc speaks from the rear of the audience, or over a speaker system. It's
his most human moment.

Have you ever remembered the moment you fell asleep on any given night? A
few minutes before, maybe—or even a few moments after. But the exact
moment that divides asleep from awake—never. My mother keeps trying to
remember that moment. She says that if she can remember that moment—if
she can just capture that moment—she'll have a handle on death.

The music of bells begins again, as the two on stage dance with one another.

ONE

You're so beautiful.

ANOTHER

You. You're so beautiful.

ONE

You. While they're watching?

ANOTHER

Who?

ONE

Them—oh.

ANOTHER

Are you…are you mad?

ONE

I feel I am.

ANOTHER

While they're watching?

ONE

When I was young, I would hear voices in the thunder.

ANOTHER

I would see faces in the branches against my bedroom window.

ONE

You're so beautiful.

ANOTHER

You.

ONE

Is this acting?

ANOTHER

Is this dialogue?

ONE

Are we alive?

ANOTHER

Have we ever been more alive?
Are you breathing?

ONE

Can you feel me breathing?

ANOTHER

I was taught in school that God created all creatures male and female.

ONE

So, God was divisive from the start.

ANOTHER

And that Adam was jealous of the love the beasts and birds could express to
one another.

ONE

So, rather than let Adam learn to love himself, this God stepped in, split
Adam in two and said here—love something outside yourself.

ANOTHER

That is not how I learned it, but yes. Yes.

ONE

I was taught in school that the greatest contribution to modern mathematics
was the concept of zero. I never knew zero 'til now.

ANOTHER

Then zero must be the point where people and their ideas move out beyond
their boundaries to become their opposites.

ONE

That is not how I learned it, but yes. Yes.

ANOTHER

Are we acting?

ONE

Is this dialogue?

ANOTHER

Do we have time?

ONE

While they're watching?

ANOTHER

Are you…are we mad?

ONE

Most likely.

ONE AND ANOTHER

Then breathe.

They embrace again, breathing together. Doc Grinder enters, once again male.
Unnoticed, he tip-toes over to them and mimics their ballet-like movements.

DOC GRINDER

Well, what's up, said doc.
What's comin' down.
How's tricks?
What's…

He laughs, realizing what he must do.

DOC GRINDER

What's in a name!

He snaps his fingers, the music stops, and the two break apart, each more clearly gender-identified and individuated. As they are named, each becomes solidly the other gender. Doc walks into the audience, sitting in an aisle to watch the rest of the scene.

KATE/HERMAN

What's your name?

ABEL

Abel.

KATE/HERMAN

You're a man?

ABEL

Does it matter?

KATE/HERMAN

It's beginning to.

ABEL

Your name is…?

KATE

Kate.

ABEL

Then you're becoming a man?

KATE

I'm becoming a woman.

ABEL

Is this acting?

KATE

Seems like it.
Is this dialogue?

ABEL

Yes.

They exit separately.

DOC GRINDER

Walks back up to the stage. He is not untouched by their separation.

Neither shall remember having danced with the other.
Fragments—sketches—bits of this moment
shall return to each in their dreams.
But hey—hey, Perfesser!
Gimmee that old postpartum rag!

He snaps his fingers. Piano version of Gershwin's **Rialto Ripples Rag**.

Act II, Scene 7

COOK

*In the original production, the Cook was played by the Herman/Kate actor,
á la Julia Child. She manipulates a large wad of bread dough, shaped like
a penis, using a variety of surgical instruments. The words she speaks are
verbatim from my surgeon's report.*

Under general anesthesia after routine pre operative preparation and drap-
ing, the patient was placed in the lithotomy position. Penile inversion technique genital conversion surgery is accomplished. Incision was made over

the scrotum in the midline. The scrotal skin and...

CLERK

In the original production, the Clerk was played by the actor playing Herculine/Abel. The words he speaks are verbatim translations of the actual civil record in the case of Herculine Barbin.

By the judgment of the civil court Saint-Jean d'Angely, dated 21 June 1860, it has been ordained that the birth record of Herculine Barbin should be rectified in this sense...

COOK

Then with finger dissection, we continued to form the large vaginal cavity. Once this was done, a large pack was placed in the area, and we returned to the penile skin, into which we placed a plastic tube, while the lower third of the penile skin was completely denuded. This was to act as a skin graft within the vaginal cavity. The posterior aspect of the orifice was accomplished primarily with chromic catgut sutures utilizing...

CLERK

Amendment one—that the first name Abel shall be substituted for the first name Herculine...

COOK

We then tailored a labia majora, excising out the excessive scrotal skin, and returned to the before-mentioned purse-string suture which was now pursed in such a fashion as to not obliterate the blood supply but as to purse the new clitoris in an outward direction. The patient withstood the procedure well and returned to the recovery ward in good condition.

She places a small birthday candle in the vagina-shaped dough, and lights it.

CLERK

Amendment two—that the child registered here will be designated as being of the masculine sex. So the record shall stand in the case of Abel Barbin.

Blackout. The two characters exit in the dark.

ACT II, Scene 8

A single spotlight comes up on Doc, still male, seated on his stool.

DOC GRINDER

We wouldn't leave you hanging there. Let's give these kids—what? Three years? Sure—time enough for them to discover that there is no acceptance for their kind—not one hundred years ago, and certainly not today. And so—three years have passed.

Believe it. Hey—trust me!

He exits as the lights go down. Deep-toned church bells sound.

ACT II, Scene 9

ABEL

Walks onto the stage, dressed in black with a white shawl. He is in a grave-yard, speaking to the tombstones.

I was such a fool to have believed! To have trusted! To have obeyed! To have thought I would have enjoyed this. Who were you with such a grand stone? Cardinal Lefevre! How fitting that you lie there and I tread upon your bones. Tell me, Cardinal, tell me now that you are beyond it all—tell me what are the rules. Tell me how I, raised to be passed from father to husband, from one man to another—tell me how I am to be a man! How would you know—you got into skirts just as soon as you could.

Something I cannot recall about the significance of zero.

Oh, Grandfather, Poppy—you and your sister were the only two who let me be the preposterous woman that I was. It mattered not to you. Grandpappa—I am not a successful man. I spent my life in a world of women—the only men I knew were the priests and you, Poppy.

Excuse my deplorable manners—how is your new neighbor, who? Ah yes, Captain Bordeaux! Good evening, Captain. Tell me, grandfather—is the distinguished captain scandalized by me? Most of Paris is.

The incessant struggle between nature and reason exhausts me more and more each day, and drags me with great strides toward the tomb. It is no longer years that remain to me but months, days, perhaps. I feel that in an obvious, terrible way, and how sweet, how consoling this thought is for my soul. Death is there. Oblivion, there. There without any doubt the poor wretch exiled from the world, shall at last find a homeland, brothers, friends. And there, too, shall the outlaw find a place.

Grandpappa—can you recall the moment of your death? I cannot even recall the moment I fall asleep, though I try and try. Is death like that moment? I believe my mother always wondered about that.

He kneels, placing the white scarf on the tombstone. He addresses either the audience or the other graves, or both.

Can any of you tell me the answer to that? Can any of you tell me how I can be a man when I am both man and woman? Can any of you light a candle for me?

Lights fade to black, the church bells toll slowly, as he walks off stage.

ACT II, Scene 10

Cold lights come up to reveal Doc in top hat and tails, walking downstage toward the spot where Abel had just been. He begins to kneel, but catches himself, watching the audience warily. He struggles with the decision, then kneels to the scarf, slowly picking it up, his face contorted with grief. He buries his face in the scarf. He slowly rises, pulling the scarf away from his face, revealing a hideous grin. Music in: Disco version of **Ding Dong The Witch is Dead** *by Klaus Nomi. He laughs.*

DOC GRINDER

It's Party Time!

He moves into the audience, speaking to them over the music. He directs these lines to different audience members.

Hey—I told you to defend your gender—but you wouldn't listen, and now there's Hell to pay!!! Now you—you look like you could use two bottles of blue, am I right? Of course I'm right! I've got a special for you—four bottles for the price of five—you'll love it!

And you—I've been looking at you all evening, and I still can't figure you out—what'll it be, pink or blue?

Kate enters, fully female now, and cuts music off abruptly with a sharp whistle.

DOC GRINDER
HEY! HEY, YOU CAN'T STOP THE SHOW LIKE THAT!

KATE
I just did.

DOC GRINDER
I'll have you written out of the show! I'll have you replaced! There's plenty of freaks like you in this town.

KATE
Go ahead—make my day.

DOC GRINDER
Not very womanly, are we?

KATE

Striking an overly-"feminine" pose.

Maybe not.

DOC GRINDER
And certainly not much of a man.

KATE
Maybe I'm neither.

DOC GRINDER

Oh NO! You answered all these questions!

KATE

Maybe my answers bred new questions. New rules to break. New lines to cross.

She goes over to Doc's stool, and sits down on it.

DOC GRINDER

Absolutely delighted that she is about to make a fool of herself.

And you want the stage? Go ahead ! Make my day ! Go ahead.

He strides into the audience, sitting down to watch what she does.

Act II, Scene 11

KATE

She picks up a candle from Herculine's night stand, and lights it.

Abel died an artful death. He shut all the windows in his flat and turned on the gas from every possible fixture. An artful death at his own hands. Death and gender were once the property of the individual. Soon they were taken over by the community, the church, the medical profession, the state. His was not a medicalized death. It was then *(blowing out candle)* art.

Something I don't remember about the significance of zero.

Doc Grinder laughs abruptly from the audience.

As to being a man or a woman, must I be one or the other? Must you? Do you know what one is, or the other?

DOC GRINDER

Moving rapidly back to reclaim the stage. Grandly.

A man has a penis!

KATE

I'm constructing myself to be fluidly gendered now.

DOC GRINDER

A woman has…

He searches for the right word. Kate waits, expectantly.

DOC GRINDER

…no penis!

KATE

Do you know what you're constructing?

DOC GRINDER

Men have sex with women.

KATE

Because you and I are constructing our gender nearly every waking moment.

DOC GRINDER

Women have sex with men.

KATE

I need to be aware of constructing my gender, that's all.

DOC GRINDER

I can have all this enforced in any court in the land!

KATE

Oh really? Well, I used to have a cock, and now I don't. I have a cunt. And I still fuck women, and women still fuck me. If the right man came along, I might fuck him.

I don't consider myself a man, and quite frequently I doubt that I'm a woman. And you—you still think gender is the issue! Gender is not the issue. Gender is the battlefield. Or the playground. The issue is us versus them. Any us versus any them. One day we may not need that.

But, today? I live well, if underground. Nowadays, when I sit alone in my father's chair, sometimes I leave a quarter. Sometimes I don't.

I've said my piece, and I feel...curiously relieved. I feel fulfilled. You work out the rest, if you have the energy for it. The outlaw has found her place.

She turns and exits.

Act II, Scene 12

DOC GRINDER

He is stunned, turns to face audience, and begins to applaud.

Bravo! Bravo! Bra—Brava!!! BRAVA! It gets very confusing, doesn't it?!? Wonderful words—just...wonderful words.

To the departed Kate.

Don't expect any federal funding for them though!

To the audience.

I know what you're thinking. You're thinking that he...she...oh let's just say she, shall we? You're thinking that...she...made...her point. Good point, too. Damned good point. In theory.

But that's got nothing to do with you and me.

I'll tell you something—we're going to go home tonight, you and I—

and before we fall asleep we're going to say, thank heavens at least I'm a man. Thank heavens, at least I'm a woman. They can't say that!

Grinder's theme music back in. He laughs in triumph.

But you say you're a bit unsettled by all this? You say you need some help? I say I've got it for you—in the pink and blue bottles! You just come see me backstage. Thank you—so much—for coming this evening.

CURTAIN

Maggie, the goddess-in-training, in the first production of **The Opposite Sex is Neither**, directed by Iris Landsberg.

ALBERT
HERMAN

the punchline

It was right around the time I started writing this book that my female lover, Catherine, became my boyfriend, David. It was right around that time that everything I'd been thinking about gender got thrown back into the blender. And that really made me think. That really made me throw up my hands and say, "Here we go again!"

The Opposite Sex is Neither at P. S. 122, New York City, 1993, directed by Iris Landsberg.

« 16 »

THE SEVEN YEAR ITCH
(What Goes Around, Comes Around)

I remember reading somewhere that it takes seven years for the human body to regenerate itself completely. That means in one seven year period, every cell in our bodies dies, and is replaced by a new cell. So the body you are wearing right now probably hasn't got one cell in common with the body you were wearing, say, seven years and six months ago.

As a species, we die and rebirth ourselves every seven years.

Now, this has some very interesting implications for a person like me. This past May, May 1st, I reached the seventh anniversary of my genital conversion surgery. That's what they call it now when they wanna be polite. It's what we all mean when we say "the surgery."

As in, "When did you get the surgery?"
Or, "Are you going to have the surgery?"
Or, "How much did the surgery cost you?"
The surgery is where they laid out my penis out on a table,
slit it up the middle
and gutted it like a fish out of water,
then sewed it up
and poked it back up inside me,
kinda like turning a sock inside-out.
And this is my vagina.
Same cells, different cell-block.

Man-made.
So seven years have gone by,
since the surgery
and all these cells I'm wearing
and all these cells I'm bearing
and all these cells I'm being
they're all brand-new.
Technically speaking, this body is homegrown.
Just like yours.
Ninety-nine and forty-four one-hundredths percent pure.
Like the Ivory girl.
Maybe we belong to the same club after all.
You and me.

> See,
> I keep looking for that club
> I keep looking for a home
> I keep checking out the rollbooks
> And I haven't found my family name anywhere.
> I keep looking for the uniforms
> I keep listening for the anthem
> I wanna learn the right dance step
> But my family's been carded at the door
> And anyway,
> If they let us dance,
> Me and my people,
> If they let us dance,
> Who would lead?

Growing up, I would read these books. They all had passages like:

*I couldn't wait for Aunt Peg and Lisa to leave
the house. I immediately went into Lisa's
room. My heart was pounding. I went to
Lisa's dresser looking for her underwear.
When I pulled open her lingerie drawer,*

I just stopped and stared in silence as I gently pulled out her panties, bra, slips and other items one at a time and held each in front of my naked body. I slipped into a pair of panties along with a bra I'd stuffed with tissues. I then pulled on a beige half slip. Seeing myself in the mirror was so exciting and just as I was beginning to rub my silken encased penis, I was shocked by Lisa's voice saying, "well which of my dresses are you going to wear."

—Anonymous, *The Male Majorette*,

c. 1967

In the erotica of my people, we are always discovered.
Discover me.

In the '60s, when I was a hippie boy, I really believed the Beatles and Alan Watts and Kahlil Gibran and I guess even the Maharishi that love was all you need.

My hair was longer then than it is now.

I wore beads and bellbottoms.

I said things like *Far Out* and *Groovy.*

All the people around me were in the peace movement.

But I never really understood the peace movement

because I never understood

peace.

I was too much at

war

with myself, I guess,

and I never got close enough to the war inside me

to compare it to the war that was going on all around me.

Like the guy who lives up the block from me now. We're at war, he and I.

He hangs out getting drunk with the street people in front of the video store across from the Safeway. He follows me home.

If I'm walking out my door and he's nearby, he'll say, "Mmmmm, just in time." I made the mistake of smiling at him the first day. He said, "Wanna suck on those tits, bitch."

Seven years and six months ago, these breasts weren't around to get me in trouble like that.

Now, he comes up to me if I stay in my car too long.

He licks his lips.

He rubs his hand over his crotch.

My mother never raised me to deal with this.

I haven't spent my lifetime learning how to deal with this.

Each time I see him, I feel like a deer on the highway, caught in the headlights of an oncoming truck.

Fifteen years after my hippie boy stage

(or two complete bodies later, depending on how you're gonna calculate time),

when I went through with my gender change,

when I had the surgery,

when they raised and lowered that knife,

when they cut through the blood and bone and nerve,

I thought to myself now I'm gonna know some peace of mind.

When they picked up a needle and thread

and sewed me back together again,

I said to myself Now I'm gonna find my contentment.

And when I lay there healing and the pain was so intense

that all I could do was keep on crying,

I said to myself, the war is over,

let's build myself a memorial to the dead.

But it didn't work out that way.

There were still wars going on in my brain.

I wonder what makes these little cells so smart? I mean, you'd think if they'd once formed a penis, they might recombine into *another* penis after seven years. But nope. Nope. They do what they last remember having been. These little cells remember to reform themselves into a vulva and vagina, such as mine are.

And what about those dead and dying cells…the ones that disappear?

No one talks about *them*. Where do *they* go?

> Somewhere, out there, there's a complete dead man's body, disassembled into micro-units—like those transporters do on Star Trek? Beam me up, Scotty. There's no life for me down here.

Somewhere, over the last seven years of my life, I left behind me all the cells that add up to a body out there that looked remarkably like this one, like the one I built with the food I would eat and the alcohol I would drink in order to avoid dealing with my life.

> Look at me
> All of me
> My transsexual body is going on display
> Wednesdays through Sundays
> at Josie's Cabaret and Juice Joint
> Come one, come all and
> Look at me.
> These breasts are real y'know, I grew 'em myself.
> This vagina cost more than the car I drive
> But only if you don't include insurance
> and I've got the no-fault kind
> the cheap kind
> I'm an assigned risk
> Hey!
> These stretch marks are real too
> I got 'em by being the fat kid in grade school
> See, I ate my way through all my questions
> It was them or me and my questions were eating me
> day and night.
> My questions stayed down deep
> Right down there with my comfort
> My questions were chewing on my heart while I chewed on
> my Hostess twinkies
> my M&Ms

my red licorice
and grandma's chicken fricassee
I chewed it all and I never tasted a bite.
All I could taste was my burning heart.

I never stopped reading those porn books.
I still have a small collection of them.

"Oh my God," said Faye as she buried her face in her hands. "What are we going to do now?"

"I have a little plan for our friend Frank here," Helen laughed. It was an unpleasant laugh. "He's been snooping around and asking so many questions that he's really gotten on my nerves. After what he did to you down on the beach, Faye, I can bring charges of immoral conduct against him, and..." she paused, then continued menacingly, "I have a picture to prove it."

"What do you want me to do?" I said, sitting down on the boudoir chair.

"Well," she replied, her voice as cold as the steel of the Magnum she held, "Well, since you are so interested in women, I think you should be given an opportunity to learn more about them—more completely—from the inside out, you might say. You'll have to learn to respect women and the best way to learn is through direct experience. Mr. Frank Martin, you will take the place of Mildred, the maid, for the next three days. If you satisfy us, we will tear up the photo and never say a word about what you tried to do to Faye."

She must be kidding, I thought. Me, as a

girl? Ridiculous! But then I looked down the
barrel of the gun she was leveling directly at
me. "I'll...I'll d-do anything you say," I said,
frightened.
  "Oh goodie," giggled Faye, waving her gun.
She was overjoyed.
                    —Anonymous, *The Case Of The*
                      Accidental Murder, c. 1962

In the erotica of my people, we're nearly always forced into our
change.
    I guess I was forced into it.
    I guess you might call the pornography a force.
    I guess you might call all the advertising a force.
    You might call the doctors who kept telling me
    that if I wasn't a man I had to be a woman,
    you might call them a force.
    You might call the fashion industry a force.
    On the other hand,
    you might call forcing someone to be one gender or another,
    you might call that
    a fashion.

                          I am not a man.
                          I am not a woman.
                          I like playing.
                          I've always loved make-believe!
                          Of all the options I've got, I like being girl the best.

    I grew this body.
    It's a girl body.
    All of it.
    Over the past seven years every one of these cells became girl,
    so it's mine now.
    It doesn't make me female.
    It doesn't make me a woman.

And I'm sure not a man.
What does that make me?

"Wanna suck those tits, bitch."

I'm supposed to be writing about how to be a girl. I don't know how to be a girl. And I sure don't know how to be a boy. And after thirty-seven years of trying to be male and over eight years of trying to be female, I've come to the conclusion that neither is really worth all the trouble. And that made me think. A lot of people think it *is* worth the trouble. And that made me think. Why? Why do people think it's worth all that trouble to be a man? Why do people think it's worth all that trouble to be a woman? And hey, I'm not just talking about transsexuals here. I'm talking about men and women, maybe like you. I am so intensely curious about what it must feel like to be convinced you're a man. I'm sitting here tapping this out on my computer, and I'm thinking about who might be reading this; and I know that some of you really believe you are women. I want to get down on my knees in front of you, I want to get down on my knees, and I want to look up into your eyes and I want to say tell me! Tell me what it's like!

> The tall red-haired actress drops to her knees downstage center. She looks up at the audience, her face framed in an amber spotlight. "Tell me what it's like to know you're a woman," she says, her voice barely raised above a whisper. "Tell me what it's like to know you're a man. Tell me please because I never went to bed one night of my life knowing I was a man. I never went to bed one night of my life knowing I was a woman."

My favorite book in our house when I was growing up was the dictionary. We had this huge dictionary. It was the size of a million phone books. It had its own pedestal in the hallway of our house. And it had its own light on the wall, aimed right down on the tan leather cover and the gold-leaf edged pages. And when you turned on the light, it would shine down on that dictionary, and after a little while under the direct light, the leather binding would get warm, and give off an intoxicating scent that I would inhale every time I came to look up a word, whenever I needed to know what something meant. I've come to associate the meaning of all the important things in my life with the smell of warm leather.

When I was little, and I would say to my parents, what does this word mean, they would say, "Go look it up in the dictionary, Albert." And I would run, I would run flying to that corner of the hallway, to get my daily shot of leather and truth.

> I think I always knew there was sex in that book. But I had far too much respect for its aging and brittle pages to come right out and say, excuse me, could you please tell me what I'm supposed to do with this thing hanging down between my legs? I mean, what would I do if it told me I was supposed to keep that thing? No, it was better not to look at all, I thought. So I never looked up sex. I let her sleep in the dictionary somewhere between self-analysis and shady.

I looked in other pages for Sex.

The dictionary was the first taste I ever got of The Information Age. It had information I needed. It had information I wanted. That dictionary had information I craved. I believed with all my heart that the dictionary in our hallway would tell me who I was, what I was, if only I could read it right.

And that's how I discovered The Information Age.
See, I wanted to be informed.
I wanted to be in the know.
I wanted the hall light on and somebody home.
I wanted to be clued in.
I wanted to be in the loop.
I wanted to wear a knowing smile.
I wanted to wear that smile like a beacon.
I wanted people to look at my smile and say

There goes a girl who knows what she wants
There goes a girl who knows her way around
I wanted people to look at me and say
There goes an Information Age girl.
But I was too busy for the Information Age
When I was a boy.
I was too busy eating, drinking, fucking, smoking, spending, gambling
my way away from the information I needed.

And so I gave that shit up. I just put it aside.
I just said no.
One day at a time.
Easy does it.
First things first.
Honk if you're a friend of Bill W.
I shed my addictions like a snake sheds its skin.
I shed my addictions 'til I got down to
who I thought I really was
shivering naked it was just me left
me and who I thought I was.
And one by one I shed who I thought I was too,
all the who's I thought I really was.
I am shedding my identities
like I shed my dead and dying cells.
And every time I open the dictionary,
and find my picture next to one of those words.
I tear the page out of the dictionary and I
swallow it whole
and I shit it out
that's what I do when they try to label me now.
I am tearing pages out of the dictionary.
Imagine my surprise when the next page I hadda tear out,
the page that was hanging around my neck,
the page I'd held close to my heart all this time,
so close it was choking me and I didn't know it
Imagine my surprise when I had to destroy

the page with the word Lesbian written on it.

> There's an old Jewish proverb: God created people because God loves good stories. Wanna real good one? OK, here we go.

See,
My Girlfriend is becoming the man of my dreams.
She is becoming the man my mother always wanted me to be.
Catherine has become David.
Like the old button from the '60s:
"My Karma Ran Over My Dogma."
Can you imagine?
I wake up one morning,
A nice lesbian like me,
I wake up one morning,
and I'm living with a man!
There were some questions I didn't want to ask
and I've been having to ask them:
...could I live with a man as my lover?
and if I could do that,
...with a man as my lover, what was I?

I hadda stick around for this one.
I couldn't leave this guy.
I had to stand by my man.
Nuthin I can do,
Cuz I'm stuck like glue
to my guy!
Hey!
I can sing all those old lovesongs now,
Without changing the pronouns.

And, hey!
It keeps me moving.
See, it's been seven years since my surgery.

It's been seven years of crawling in the sun like a snake
while I shed my skin year after year after year
Trying to keep three feet ahead of the dictionary.
Trying to keep out of reach of the people who think
it's so important to be a man
Trying to keep out of reach of the people who think
it's so important to be a woman
I really don't understand those people
Do you?
I don't understand the people who want me to be a man
I don't understand the people who want me to be a woman.
Do you?
It's been seven years, and y'know what?
I still get a thrill
when I look at myself in the mirror and I see girl not boy.
It's a lark!
Girl?
It's a gas!
Girl?
It's a hoot!
Girl?
It's an identity I am working my way out of.
And by the time the next seven years have come and gone
My girl skin will be lying behind me in the desert.
Right next to my lesbian skin.
Right next to my man skin.
Right next to my boy skin.
By the time the next seven years have come and gone
I'll be the one the dictionary has trouble naming.
By the time the next seven years have come and gone
Nothing of this body is gonna be left for them to find.
Nothing of this body is gonna be around.
Get your last looks now, 'cause I'm changing already
And by the time the next seven years have come and gone
I'm gonna be new all over again.

WHOOPS . . .
THERE'S MORE TO SAY:
Afterword to the Vintage Edition

I'm so glad for the opportunity to write some words for this paperback edition of *Gender Outlaw*.

> A great deal has happened in the world outside of gender since the publication of the hardcover edition last year, and I think it's important to look at the stuff in this book in light of the newer context. Here we go!

• In May of 1994, David Harrison, a female-to-male transsexual man, wrote and performed the solo performance work *FTM: A Transsexual Journey From Female to Male* at 848 Performance Space in San Francisco, directed by Mimi McGurl. First time ever for a female-to-male voice to be heard live onstage.

• Also in May 1994 at the 848 Gallery, Loren Cameron premiered his collection of black-and-white photos of transgendered men, women, and others: *Our Vision, Our Voices: Transsexual Portraits and Nudes*. It was the first exhibit of photos taken by a transsexual person.

• In September of 1994, Barbara Reumüller and DV8-Film produced *TranSEX*, the world's first transgender film festival in Vienna, Austria.

• In October 1994, Tim Miller and Jordan Peimer of Highways Performance Space in Santa Monica, California, produced *TransFusion*, the world's first transgender performance art festival.

• Articles appeared in both *The New Yorker* and *Details* magazines this past year about the female-to-male side of the coin, which comprises (not surprisingly) roughly 50 percent of the transgender population.

• In February 1995, *Apartheid of Sex: A Manifesto on the Freedom of Gender*, by Martine Rothblatt, was published by Crown Publishers.

> Rothblatt, herself a transsexual lesbian, has compiled an astounding volume of facts and figures, and has put forth a heartfelt call to dismantle the oppressive gender system under which we live. We agree on many points, she and I; and what I love about that is that we were both developing these ideas, writing these books of ours before we'd ever met!

• The Ingersoll Center in Seattle, Washington, founded by Marsha Botzer in 1984, is as far as I know the only counseling center for gender care in the world that is run and staffed mostly by transgendered people. Plans are underway to make their staff available worldwide through online computer services.

• Leslie Feinberg, author of the amazing book *Stone Butch Blues* (which won several awards and is being read more and more *and* is soon to be a motion picture), is emerging as the political leader of this transgender culture of ours.

> I'm eyeing the job of her court jester.

• Even television shows are shifting gears. In my third appearance on

Geraldo, I was a guest expert! It was a show called "The War Between the Sexes." They must have figured I was Switzerland.

> We're moving from perverts to experts in that venue, those of us who are speaking out, telling our stories. The next step will be when these shows take on a panel of us non-gendered folks talking about the nature of identity in this culture.

• I included my e-mail address in the first edition of this book (OutlawGal@AOL.com), and I've been getting a lot of mail: sometimes five to ten letters a day. I do answer all of 'em … it just takes me some time. The responses from other transgendered folks range from thank-you's, to heated disagreement, to outpourings of their own stories. The next largest group of folks who write say things like "I'm not a *transsexual* woman, but I have to create myself as a woman every day of my life, and I know what you're talking about!" That is so gratifying to hear. And there are a number of letters from men who say, "I'm not transsexual or a gay man, but I've felt trapped in MAN for a long time." Bingo.

• *Gender Outlaw* has already gone through two hardcover printings. I understand it's now on reading lists at many colleges and universities. Thanks go to Bill, Stuart, Vicki, Jonathan, and Eric and the folks at Routledge for their courage and foresight in first publishing this book, and for their decision to toss the ball to Vintage, which is making this more affordable edition available.

So that's some of the year in review. More of our own voices are out in the world. Blows me away. I really think our time has come. It's going to be a long road ahead, but we're moving. We're moving in the direction of establishing a space in this world that exists outside of the socially sanctioned gender system, what the writer Caitlin Sullivan calls "the two-gender system." We're out of the closet and we've got a foothold in this world as ourselves.

Wait! I *Should* Have Said . . .

When I sat down to write this book, my worst fear was that these ideas would be frozen in time: that I'd change my mind, re-look at stuff and have to pull back on some points; but that this book would be on the shelf, staring back at me, carved in stone. I tried very hard to phrase as much as I could in terms of questions, which would outlast my own opinions about the answers. Well, I made some statements and omissions that I'd like to amend.

When I talk about therapists in this book, I go overboard. I generalized some of my own experience and knowledge about the therapy experience, which in a nutshell was: "Hey, you're either a man or a woman." Several therapists have since approached me, assuring me that not all therapists buy into the bipolar trap, and that not all therapists recommend to their clients that they lie about their transgender status. I'm so relieved to hear that, and I want to make the point that these are the kinds of caregivers we need to approach for our support.

I use the term "non-operative" (or "non-op") transsexual in this book to refer to people who don't feel that genital surgery is necessary to living an other-gendered life. The term needs to be credited to Markisha Greaney, a transsexual woman who wrote an extensive paper on that subject way before I thought of writing *Gender Outlaw*.

I use the term *shaman* to describe the more spiritual identity experienced by those who go through major transitions in their lives. It's a term from other cultures, and I don't want to weaken the strength and passion of that experience as lived in communities outside our own repressed Eurocentric culture. We need to come up with a new term for the way we experience that.

I also refer to myself as a "lesbian." Well, I'm not too sure about that one these days. See, I live my life *as* a woman in my day-to-day walking around, but I'm not under any illusion that I *am* a woman. I love people who live their lives as women in this world: I'm way attracted to people who do that, it's in their direction that I want to push my support. But that doesn't make me a "lesbian." There's a whole lesbian world out there that doesn't quite ring true with the culture that transgendered people are finally beginning to carve out for ourselves. As Leslie Feinberg points out, we are different cultures, lesbians/gays and the transgendered, and we overlap at some points. I'm living my life *as* a lesbian, with many similarities to some lesbians, but I'm not under the illusion that I *am* a lesbian. It's the difference between *being* an identity and *having* an identity. The latter makes more room for individual growth, I think.

And finally, I make reference to Arnold Schwarzenegger doing impeccable male drag, and I say that he doesn't have a sense of humor about it. Well, . . . as I'm writing this, I see that he's done a film in which his macho male character gets himself pregnant! Haven't seen it yet, but, Arnold: you go, girl!

> Who knows, maybe some brave television producer will actually soon write for and cast a true transsexual to play a transsexual person as an ongoing character in some TV series. (Major hint . . . my résumé is ready, Mr. Bochco.)

New Questions

I've been tramping around the world, doing lectures, book readings, online interviews, radio and TV talk shows, symposiums, and panels, as well as performances of my two solo pieces, *The Opposite Sex Is Neither* and *Virtually Yours, a Game for Solo Performer with Audience.* I try to build in as many question-and-answer sessions as possible everywhere I go because I think that's the key: asking our own questions about our own issues. Some questions have come up, good ones, that I didn't address in the hardcover edition of *Gender Outlaw.*

"Why, if you knew all this, if you knew that gender was a construct and didn't depend on biology and, more specifically, genitalia, did you go ahead with your genital surgery?"

"The answer is simple: I didn't know all this stuff before my genital surgery. I bought into the two-gender system like most everyone else. It was only six months later when some women asked me "How can you be a woman the same way *we're* women?" that I began to question the two-gender system.

"And if you knew what you know now, would you do it again?"

Big-time yes! I think I might have gone ahead even more carefully than I did, but knowing what I know about having this vagina and vulva, I'm very glad I did what I did. I've come to see a difference, though, between a penis and the phallus. The former, as it is so wonderfully acknowledged in the film *The Crying Game*, is merely a "flap of flesh." The phallus is another story. I see the phallus as a symbol of a misuse of power in this world, one that has become linked to penises. More and more transgendered people are either refusing to take on a phallus (female-to-male) or are deconstructing their own phallus, but leaving their penises intact (male-to-female).

"Why are the female-to-male transsexuals less visible?"

Several reasons. First, they pass better, generally. And that has a lot to do with the tendency in this culture to attribute "male" to an ambiguously gendered person. (See Kessler and McKenna's book, *Gender: An Ethnomethodological Approach*, for an in-depth study of the phenomenon of gender attribution, and its inherent phallocentricity.)

Second, there is a culturally imposed male silence, an idea that "real men don't talk about their feelings." In their efforts to be "real men," some FTM transsexual men do buy into that silence. Thankfully, leaders like James Green, David Harrison, Jason Cromwell, and Loren Cameron don't buy into male stereotyping, and they're making it safe for others to follow suit.

Lastly, I think that female-to-male transsexuals are more dangerous to the two-gender system. In this misogynist culture, it's easy to look at someone like me and laugh. "He's stepped down a notch to become a woman," goes the sexist reasoning. "He's a clown." But when someone comes forward, with or without a penis, and says "I am a man," whoa! There's a new kind of man being birthed in this culture, a new kind of masculinity being born out of a feminist sensibility, in many cases out of a lesbian sensibility. I love these new men! And they are way dangerous to the guys who still grunt and scratch, aren't they? Unfortunately the latter use their power to silence these new men in most of our media. But that's changing.

"So what you're saying, Kate, is that none of us has a gender, and we're all equal?"

Sort of, kind of. But there's a danger in that way of thinking, in the same way that there is a danger to any humanist philosophy. The fact is, the two-gender system exists. The vast majority of the world buys into it. And so much violence is done to women in the confines of that system. The Women's Movement is the front line now. The struggle to end the oppression of women, and the violence done to women *must* take global priority. What I'm proposing in this book is sorta like the guy who sweeps up the parade route after the elephants have gone by. What I'm proposing, after the violence is checked, is that we dismantle the system that has held it in place for so long.

> Not a question, but a comment I got from a man who attended a reading of *Gender Outlaw* in Hartford, Connecticut. "My grandmother," he said, "told me something I've never forgotten. 'Never fuck anyone you wouldn't want to be.'" The room went silent for a long time.

And lastly, "How do you *live* without gender?"

I look for where gender is, and I go someplace else. Kind of like the old saw about learning how to fly? You throw yourself at the ground, and miss. I'm writing a new book now, more of a practical thing. The working title is, *My Gender Workbook: A Practical Guide for Becoming a Man, a Woman, or Something Else Entirely.* Should be fun.

So with all the above stuff in mind, I'm very happy with this edition of *Gender Outlaw.* I'm looking forward to more and more transgendered voices being raised in this culture, the whole rainbow of us. And I'm looking forward to the day when people look at this book and say to themselves, "How curious to have to put all that energy into talking about gender. I wonder what the world must have been like in those days for folks with only two choices."

—Kate Bornstein
December 1994

ACKNOWLEDGMENTS

I want to thank the people who've helped me travel as far as I have.

With special love and gratitude to my mother, Mildred Bornstein, who has put up with an awful lot from me. From my mother, I learned how to be gracious under fire, how to look for the laughter in any situation, and, most importantly, how to say no, when no must be said.

You kept the love there through all the hard times. Thank you, mom.

Thanks so much to Rose Pascarell at George Mason University, who first told me I should write this book, who nursed me through the fear and trepidations of it all, who read it in its shoddier stages, and with whom I was able to spend some of the more wonderful times of my life.

And to my friend, Alice Zander, who taught me the principle that someone's life's work begins at the point where their great joy meets the world's great hunger. She also taught me what to do with my pocketbook at restaurants, and other neat femme-y stuff like that.

Thanks to Holly Hughes: your work inspired me to write at all, and I'm in awe of your talent and your courage.

With gratitude to the women of Split Britches—Lois Weaver, Peggy Shaw, and Deb Margolin—who taught me that there can be so much heart in camp.

Thanks and love also to Daniel Mangin, my editor at *The Bay Area Reporter*, who brought me out as a writer; to Noreen Barnes who helped me birth *Hidden: A Gender* in writing and on stage; and to Amy Scholder who kept encouraging me to write in my own style.

To Sandy Stone, Caroline Cossey, Leslie Feinberg, Renee Richards, Rikki Ann Wilchins, Virginia Prince, Jan Morris, and Canary Conn, my deepest appreciation for blazing a trail through the virtual forest of gender.

Jim Barnhill and Don Wilmeth, for teaching me my theater skills at Brown University. Your continued faith has been a blessing.

To Suzanne Badoux, who showed me that politics could have a sense of humor.

To Rhonda Blair, who first lured me to an academic conference to present a paper on Gender and Performance.

Thanks to the following theater artists, producers and production people who've made it possible to produce *Hidden: A Gender,* and/or helped me with the time to write this book: Karen Rosenfeld, Rebecca Kaplan, John Killacky, Eleanor Savage, Thomas Mulready, Lisa Rofel, Tim Jones, Sky Gilbert, Gwen Bartleman, Mark Russell, Susan Finque, Rick Rankin, Michael Kearns, Tim Miller, Jordan Peimer, Wendy Chapkis, Gabrielle, Bruce Lee, Del Rey, Howie Baggadonutz, Jane Hill, Ron Ehmke, Donald Montwill, Vicki Wolf, Chris Rushton, Stephanie Weisman, Laura Brun, Marina Shoup, Margie Ekeberg, Will Wilkins, and Catherine Blinder.

Thanks be to whomever handed down the Macintosh computer to Apple, and the tablets of word processing to Microsoft. Special thanks to Steve Zagerman and Carol Oppenheimer of Bananafish Software, for the great program, *ThoughtPattern,* in which I made and kept all my notes for this book. And to Mona Helfgott and Chuck Nadell at Inspiration Software for their indispensable program, *Inspiration,* which I used to rough out and outline the book.

My appreciation to the Women In Theatre Program of the Association of Theater in Higher Education Conference, for showing me there could be a balance between theory and practice of theater.

Bless also my friends Linda Donald, Nicole Grimmer, Ingrid Wilhite, Stewart Wilson, Lisa Farmer, Iris Landsberg, KayLynn Raschke, Caitlin Sullivan, Cynthia Bologna, Lourdes Tallet, Flo Camponile, Loren Cameron and Isabella Radsna, and Lynn Ablondi for putting up with frantic calls at all hours, and for my neglect of their company for long months.

Thanks to my fellow Starfleet officers, especially the valiant crew of the U. S. S. Republic, for covering for me on missions I missed while preparing this book.

Thanks to Chris Kovick who booked me for a reading at Red Dora's, the text of which became the last chapter of this book.

To the original production company of *Hidden: A Gender*: Noreen Barnes, Sherry Anderson, Lori Dovi, Bobby Tyler, Rick Garlinghouse, Jill Posener, Drew Todd. A special thanks to Ken Dixon and Doug Holsclaw at Theatre Rhinoceros who commissioned *Gender*, and supported its production.

To the incredible Lori E. Seid, who was the moving force behind getting *Hidden: A Gender* out of San Francisco and onto a North American tour.

To Dona Ann McAdams, my favorite photographer—your work moves me so deeply, and I am honored to have sat for you.

To Justin Bond: thank you so much for bringing Herculine to life, and for teaching me so much about men. To Sydney Erskine, thank you for your portrayal of Herman, and for your thoughtful counsel. And thanks to Cayenne Woods for your strength in keeping the show on the road on tour.

Love and gratitude for all the support and patience; for the time and the space; and most of all, for all the magic to David Harrison, who when we first met and fell in love was Catherine Harrison, but who became David as I was writing this book, and so I've had to make room for the next book!

Thanks to Gwydyn for all the purring.

BIBLIOGRAPHY

Amadiume, Ifi. *Male Daughters, Female Husbands.* Avon: The Bath Press, 1987.

Anonymous. *The Case Of The Accidental Murder!* Tulare: Chevalier Publications, c. 1962.

Anonymous. *The Male Majorette.* Vol. Number 11. Crossdressers Fiction Series, Thompson: Echo Productions, c. 1967.

Barnes, Noreen C. A panel at The First International Lesbian and Gay Theater Conference and Festival, 1989.

Bolin, Anne. *In Search of Eve: Transsexual Rites of Passage.* New York: Bergin & Garvey, 1988.

Braindrop, Lily. "Kate Bornstein: Gender Bender/Mind Bender." *Taste of Latex*, Summer 1990.

Califia, Pat. *Sapphistry: The Book of Lesbian Sexuality.* Tallahassee: The Naiad Press, Inc., 1983.

Cameron, Loren. In personal conversation, 1993.

Chapkis, Wendy. *Beauty Secrets: Women and the Politics of Appearance.* Boston: South End Press, 1986.

Cossey, Caroline. *My Story.* Winchester: Faber and Faber, Inc., 1992.

Davis, Murray S. *Smut: Erotic Reality/Obscene Ideology.* Chicago: The University of Chicago Press, 1983.

Deikman, Arthur. *The Wrong Way Home: Uncovering Patterns of Cult Behavior in American Society.* Boston: Beacon Press, 1990.

Dibell, Dominique. Personal conversation, 1993.

Dolan, Jill. "In Defense of the Discourse: Materialist Feminism, Postmodernism, Postconstructuralism and Theory." *The Drama Review* v. 33 Number 3, Fall 1989.

Douglas, Ann. *The Feminization of American Culture.* New York: Avon, 1977.

Ehrenreich, Barbara. *The Hearts of Men: American Dreams and the Flight from Commitment.* Garden City, N. J.: Anchor Press/Doubleday, 1984.

Emigh, John. "Hajari Bhand: A Joker in the Deck." *The Drama Review* v. 30

Number 1, 1986.

Feinberg, Leslie. *Transgender Liberation: A Movement Whose Time Has Come.* New York: World View Forum, 1992.

Finque, Susan. A panel at The First International Lesbian and Gay Theater Conference and Festival, 1989.

Frazin, Jim. "Kate Bornstein: On Gender & Belonging." *Anything That Moves,* Summer, 1991.

Fussell, Paul. *Class.* New York: Ballantine Books, Random House, Inc., 1984.

Gaiman, Neil. *The Invisible Labyrinth.* Vol. 1. *The Books of Magic,* ed. Bob Kahan. New York: DC Comics, 1993.

Garber, Marjorie. *Vested Interests: Cross-Dressing and Cultural Anxiety.* New York: Routledge, 1992.

Garfinkel, Harold. *Studies in Ethnomethodology.* Englewood Cliffs, N.J.: Prentice-Hall, 1967.

Halberstam, Judith, "Queer Creatures." *On Our Backs,* Nov/Dec 1992.

Harrison, David. Personal correspondence, 1993.

Hughes, Holly. Quoted from the film, "Sphinxes Without Secrets." 1990.

Hughes, Holly. "Clit Notes." Josie's Cabaret & Juice Joint, San Francisco: 1993.

Kalweit, Holger. *Shamans, Healers, and Medicine Men.* Translated by Michael H. Kohn. Boston & London: Shambhala Publications, Inc., 1992.

Kessler, Suzanne J. and Wendy McKenna. *Gender: An Ethnomethodological Approach.* Chicago: The University of Chicago Press, 1978.

Lao-Tzu. *Tao Te Ching.* Translated by Stephen Mitchell. New York: Harper & Row, 1988.

Leslie, Jaques. "The Cursor Cowboy." *Wired,* May/June 1993.

Liette, Pierre. "Memoir of Pierre Liette on the Illinois Country." In *The Western Country in the Seventeenth Century,* ed. Milo Quaife. New York: Citadel, 1962.

Lucas, Craig. "Keynote Address." The First International Lesbian and Gay Theater Conference and Festival, 1989.

Marc, David. "Comic Visions: Television Comedy and American Culture." In *Media and Popular Culture,* ed. David Thorburn. Boston: Unwin Hyman, Inc., 1989.

Margolin, Deborah. Personal conversation, 1989.

McCarthy, Susan. "Techno-soaps and Virtual Theater." *Wired,* May/June 1993.

McDevitt, Faith. A panel at The First International Lesbian and Gay Theater Conference and Festival, 1989.

Miller, Tim. A panel at The First International Lesbian and Gay Theater Conference and Festival, 1989.

Millot, Catherine. *Horsexe / Essays on Transsexuality.* Translated by Kenneth Hylton. Brooklyn: Autonomedia, 1990.

Munk, Erika. "Representation and Its Discontents." *The Village Voice,* September 6, 1988.

Nanda, Serena. *Neither Men Nor Women: The Hijras of India.* The Wadsworth Modern Anthropology Library, ed. Peggy Adams. Belmont, California: Wadsworth Publishing Company, 1990.

Newton, Esther. *Mother Camp: Female Impersonators in America.* Chicago and London: University of Chicago Press, 1979.

Nisker, Scoop. *Crazy Wisdom.* Berkeley: Ten Speed Press, 1990.

O'Flaherty, Wendy Doniger. *Women, Androgynes, and Other Mythical Beasts.* Chicago: The University of Chicago Press, 1980.

Raymond, Janice G. *The Transsexual Empire.* Boston: Beacon Press, 1979.

Saffian, Sarah. "Kate: A Gender." *Issues Monthly,* February, 1991.

SAMOIS. "Handkerchief Codes: Interlude I." In *Coming to Power: Writings and Graphics on Lesbian S/M,* ed. SAMOIS. Boston: Alyson Publications, Inc., 1981.

Seid, Lori E. A panel at The First International Lesbian and Gay Theater Conference and Festival, 1989.

Shaw, Peggy. Personal conversation, 1989.

Starhawk. *Dreaming the Dark: Magic, Sex & Politics.* Boston: Beacon Press, 1982.

Starr, Kevin. "Indulging the Sisters." *San Francsico Examiner,* Monday, October 12, 1981.

Stone, Sandy. "The Empire Strikes Back, a Post-Transsexual Manifesto." In *Body Guards,* ed. Epstein and Straub, New York: Routledge, 1992.

Sullivan, Caitlin. Personal correspondence, 1993.

Vaughan, Diane. *Uncoupling: How Relationships Come Apart.* New York: Vintage Books, Random House, 1987.

Vidal, Gore. *Myra Breckinridge.* Boston: Bantam, 1968.

Vidal, Gore. *Myron.* New York: Ballantine Books, Random House, 1974.

Weaver, Lois. Personal conversation, 1989.

Williams, Walter L. *The Spirit and the Flesh.* Boston: Beacon Press, 1986.

Yashimoto, Banana. *Kitchen.* Translated by Megan Backus. New York: Grove Press, 1993.

THE CULTURE OF DESIRE
PARADOX AND PERVERSITY IN GAY LIVES
by Frank Browning

Nowhere has America's gay culture been observed with greater intelligence, liveliness, and sensitivity than in this provocative and deeply personal book. Taking in Cuban couples in Miami and farmers in Kentucky, AIDS activists, sexual theorists, and dedicated hedonists, *The Culture of Desire* is an intriguing insider's guide to gay America and a sharp look at the conflicts that arise when who we are is defined by whom we love.

"Absolutely cutting edge—a portrait of modern sexual politics [that] should be required reading."   —Armistead Maupin

Gay Studies/Sociology/0-679-75030-4

FAMILY VALUES
A LESBIAN MOTHER'S FIGHT FOR HER SON
by Phyllis Burke

When Phyllis Burke's lesbian partner bore a child by donor insemination, it seemed natural for Phyllis to adopt him: baby Jesse, after all, was calling her Mama. But Burke soon discovered that, even in liberated San Francisco, there were forces that would deny lesbians the legal right to be mothers.

"An important book...about motherhood, identity, honesty and love for a child. It is about homosexuals and it is pro-family. A strong challenge to prevailing 'mainstream' sensibilities."   —*Chicago Sun-Times*

Gay Studies/Sociology/0-679-75249-8

THE QUEEN'S THROAT
OPERA, HOMOSEXUALITY, AND THE MYSTERY OF DESIRE
by Wayne Koestenbaum

The Queen's Throat is at once a passionate love letter to opera and a work that triumphantly overturns our received notions of culture and sexuality. It is an innovative, profound, and wildly playful book that reveals the ways in which opera has served as a source of gay identity and gay personal style.

"[A] high-spirited and very personal book...laced with moral reflections and warmed with comedy.... A work of formidable and curious learning...a dazzling performance."   —*The New York Times Book Review*

Gay Literature/Music/0-679-74985-3

OUT IN THE WORLD
by Neil Miller

In this eye-opening and vastly entertaining book, Neil Miller travels from the black townships of South Africa to the sex clubs of Bangkok to deliver a frontline report on the lives of gays and lesbians around the world.

"Sharp, informative, and always engaging, this is first-rate work." —*The Advocate*

Vintage Departures
Gay Studies/Travel/0-679-74551-3

CLOSE TO THE KNIVES
A MEMOIR OF DISINTEGRATION
by David Wojnarowicz

David Wojnarowicz's powerful and iconoclastic memoir takes us from a violent childhood in suburbia to eventual homelessness on the streets of New York City, to recognition as one of the most provocative artists of his generation. Street life, drugs, art and nature, family, AIDS, politics, friendship and acceptance: he challenges us to examine our lives—politically, socially, emotionally, and aesthetically.

"Wojnarowicz has caught the age-old voice of the road, the voice of the traveler, the outcast, the thief, the whore, the same voice that was heard in Villon's Paris, in the Rome of Petronius. Pick up his book and listen."

—William S. Burroughs

Nonfiction/Literature/0-679-73227-6

VINTAGE ✸ BOOKS

AVAILABLE AT YOUR LOCAL BOOKSTORE, OR CALL TOLL-FREE TO ORDER: 1-800-793-2665 (CREDIT CARDS ONLY).